KC CRAMM

Ugly Happy

A Collection of Poems and Prose

Copyright © 2022 by KC Cramm

All rights reserved. No part of this publication may be reproduced, stored or transmitted in any form or by any means, electronic, mechanical, photocopying, recording, scanning, or otherwise without written permission from the publisher. It is illegal to copy this book, post it to a website, or distribute it by any other means without permission.

This novel is entirely a work of fiction. The names, characters and incidents portrayed in it are the work of the author's imagination. Any resemblance to actual persons, living or dead, events or localities is entirely coincidental.

KC Cramm asserts the moral right to be identified as the author of this work.

Designations used by companies to distinguish their products are often claimed as trademarks. All brand names and product names used in this book and on its cover are trade names, service marks, trademarks and registered trademarks of their respective owners. The publishers and the book are not associated with any product or vendor mentioned in this book. None of the companies referenced within the book have endorsed the book.

First edition

This book was professionally typeset on Reedsy.
Find out more at reedsy.com

To all of the educators who supported my work over the years with vibrant passion and dedication, especially Damon Larson, Carol Hendry, and Joseph Gardner. You inspire me and are the reason I have never stopped writing.

Also dedicated to the other members of my community who have fought for us and brought continual brightness into the world through the honesty and bravery of your existence. Thank you.

"To be in line with and to join that creativity is, I think, maybe the highest calling. I think it's all of our callings, to whatever degree or in whatever context, in whatever corner of the garden we're meant to tend. And we know it."

— Andrew Garfield

Contents

Foreword iii

I Part One

perennial bloom 3
on moving in to a haunted house 6
keloid scar 12
now i become an effigy 13
how the tide changes 15
wood music 27
a deity of some kind 28
the angel of creation manifests 29
the author's field-guide to resilience 36

II Part Two

brother by the interstate 47
the sister 50
the heart is a scared animal 51
wax + wane 52
sanctified 53
ritual of the butcher & the lamb 55
sparrow 60
moonflower (bloom of love) 62

III Part Three

the comedian jokes about transsexuals   73
hope, like a trick of the light   74
an ode to the university health clinic patient website... 76
notes on survival   81

IV Part Four

the growing-up itch   91
two mangoes   105
born artist   106
born witness   107
melody of meaningless nothing   112
hopeful, happy, ugly   121

Acknowledgments   124
About the Author   129

Foreword

This collection comprises many years of work, in an attempt to offer a summation of self and philosophy on writing. However, the vast majority of the pieces in this have been written in the past six months. They address my life as it is, right now. They are as much a breathing organ as my heart; as much a living thing as you and me.

Some of these pieces have been seen in some version by others' eyes before, through online communities and publications. Others are entirely new or are revisions of work I have edited from years past. I believe (or at least I dearly hope) that there is something in these words for everyone. *Ugly Happy* has never been just about me.

This book is not simply described, for it presents numerous abstracts and impossibilities. This book has always been about learning to reconcile the constant irregularities of life while still trying to flourish. It is a work both monumentally large and incredibly small. However I hope to offer some grace to these pieces with the following words. They are beyond me, even now. Perhaps they were never mine to begin with.

Ugly Happy is a book about growing up and finding your foothold in a world that has never seemed to fit you. It is about occupying a body that has never felt like it is yours, and learning how to live despite that. It is about grief and pain and profound loss. It is about the heart learning to forgive, even when the body cannot. It is about hurting and healing and living life as an open wound. It is about drowning within yourself because your thoughts are too loud to speak into existence. It is about profound and total loneliness. It is about hunger, consumption, and mistaking consumption for love. It is about carrying your childhood self into adulthood, no matter how heavy. It is about learning to forgive the versions of you long since gone. It is about the in-betweens, and the grey areas, and the senseless and terrifying places that seem to span forever. It is about creating art and the terrifying gift of putting art into existence.

But above all, at its heart, *Ugly Happy* is about hope, and about learning to make the world around you beautiful, even when feels an impossible task. At its root, Ugly Happy is about life that persists. "*Life sprouts best where it does not belong. Life persists, even in places marked by death. Even in graveyards, flowers bloom.*"

I do not know who will read this book. In total honesty, there's a part of me still convinced no one will. I hope that this book will reach people far from me, and I hope that the words that follow are able to offer you something meaningful. I can't think of a greater blessing than that.

I believe, above all, in the power of stories and the power of words to change people. I do not know if this book will ever accomplish something that large, but I hope, at the very least, that these words are something you can carry with you, even when this book is long since closed and collecting dust on a shelf.

That is all I can ever strive for.

I believe that writing is never done, and my work is never truly "complete." Our words evolve as we do, and the human heart grows daily. A work of writing is a perpetually growing living thing and should be given that respect. Please accept all of these pieces as evolving, breathing beings, and take them as they are.
Just like us humans, they are never finished.

I

Part One

Part One

perennial bloom

These days, I do feel happy. I can safely and proudly state that I am as happy as I have been in a long time.

Yet, this happy is not the happy I expected. This happy doesn't burn bright, singeing everything around it. Most days it is a dull sun, glowing brightly in my stomach and illuminating the inside of my ribcage in soft light, like the first few rays of morning. it does not scorch my bloodstream nor does it leave a chill. It just hangs, not bliss, not joy; just Happy.

Happy is fluid. Even when it comes and goes, I know happy will return. Happy defies all expectations. Happy makes no promises, except for the promise of presence.

Promised present occupance. I spent so long suffering; I often struggle to understand that happy is common. I expected happy to have radiance. I expected happy to be groundbreaking. I expected something earth-shattering, life-altering. Something like waking up, I suppose. New beginnings. Awakenings. Rebirth.

I expected happy to be a revolution. But this happy — this happy is held within me, familiar, known like my own bones and the marrow contained within them. Known with the familiarity of breathing and the regularity of a heartbeat.

I have come to learn that happy is a middle ground emotion, feet planted firm in the earth. Happy is grounded, level-headed.

And happy is good.

You can't be ungrateful for happy. It simply is. This happy is regular, not a tide drawn back, reaching forth and hardly touching; fingertips, outstretched between Adam and God. This happy is not a tide crashing forward, thunderous, like it could crack the earth and take us with it.

This happy is not the happy that wakes. This happy is a rhythmic sound that lulls you to sleep, reverberating in my bones like a second heart, humming in tandem alongside the universe. Measured, firm, regular.

Happy has left me shockingly still. I am still teaching myself how to breathe with the presence of happiness in my body.

Happiness, I have learned, is not radical. Not always. It blooms dull, heavy and light at the same time. Glow and fade; lightning bug yet supernova.

Happy is imperfect. Happy has questions, happy still wonders, happy still needs. Above all, happiness wants, taking root deep within bone. It wants, and it wants powerfully, to spread and grow like a weed.

I promise happiness that I am working on it. I always am. *I am planting seeds of self*, but I am a perennial flower, slow blooming. *I will take time to blossom. I will get there.* I am coming. *I promise, I am coming.*

on moving in to a haunted house

For a long time, I felt haunted.

Truth is, there is no banishing a haunting. No curing or casting it out. No force known between man or God, natural or invented, can rid a haunting.

In fact, it is much simpler than that. Easy like breathing. The only cure to a haunting is learning to live alongside it. After all, a haunting is only a reflection, even if twisted and malformed, warped and transformed into an ugly, unrecognizable body.

Beneath, there is nothing but memory.

The cure to a haunting is waiting. The cure to a haunting is held in patience and time. The cure to a haunting is filling the space. The cure to the haunting is holding it and promising, *I know you, and I see you, and I am not going anywhere.*

One can learn to live with a haunting. Even haunted houses can occupy a heart. Haunting becomes haunted becomes once was haunted – present, past, future haunted.

I accept the haunting like a childhood scar. Once painful and fresh, searing flesh, gash spilling blood and salty tears of release, white-hot pain, now familiar and permanent. I accept my scars and I occupy my haunting.

We learn to know scars. A scar is not an intrusion, a scar is not a curse, a scar is not a punishment. A scar is a memory, etched in flesh, just as a haunting is a memory etched in brick and mortar, wood and stone. The flesh of the home is not all that different than the flesh of the body; at the end of things, it deserves love and care. Without tenderness, it begins to rot, bones warping deep beneath the foundations.

Contained in the tissue that creates a scar is a promise: *the body that heals is the body that survives.* The marks are proof that you persist, despite everything. Hurt, healed, strong.

Learn to live despite the scar left behind.

We learn to love scars. I trace my old scars as if they weren't borne in pain or fear. I tell them, *you are only mine. I am only yours.* Mark of existence, promise of survival. Guaranteed continuance; proof of life etched in flesh.

In my happiness, I accept the haunting. The truth is, most ghosts ache only to be seen. It is no longer *I knew.* I know. I know. I am knowing. I am known.

I tell jokes to spirits from my youth and clutch the hands of the risen dead, holding them until they rest again. Despite their endless wails and constant screams, I learn to live alongside them. We heal our broken parts together. We have only ever belonged to each other, after all.

I have come to understand that I am a body that occupies a perennial haunting.

In this, I have learned that hauntings abandoned turn violent, but hauntings loved come to flower. Life sprouts best where it does not belong. Even in rotted, long-since abandoned houses, ivy climbs and spreads. Life persists, even in places marked by death. Even in graveyards, flowers bloom.

When the ghosts of the past return, I welcome them like old friends.

* * *

These days, I am lying in wait. Occupied by happy, kept company by ghosts. I watch seeds sprout from earth once scorched. This land, once barren, can bear life again.

In the meantime, I am familiarizing myself with my haunting. I memorize the rooms occupied by fierce specters, knife-edged bodies clawing at the walls. Even they deserve tenderness. I find the fiercest ghosts are often the most afraid; I learn to love them as I have learned to love me, and we begin to find life in this decayed and withered house.

Not all the rooms are like this. Most spirits are simply shadows burnt into the background, little more than a whisper beyond the wall. Cigarette-burn specters; so still that even ivy creeps and climbs around them. They are such wounded creatures. I've come to learn that even shadows retain bruises. I am gentle with them, too. I remind them that even a violent world can bear immense tenderness, and I show them a body that still remembers love. We find hope in each other, and we cradle each other through the nightmares.

New trucks arrive every day. I am waiting to unpack this house, this body, this life. I think of it like this: every day, I gather boxes, collected, earned, gained. Time will always accumulate new ones, filled with memories and keepsakes; new and familiar pains. I offer them all a place alongside me in the future.

In the meantime, I carry old and waterworn boxes, hauling them up the same old steps I've walked for years. They wait until they gather dust. Dust reminds of past: once lived, still carried. There is space for them, in my haunted house. I hope there is space for me, too.

I spend my long days hauling relics of myself over creaky floorboards, accompanied by familiar ghosts. I fill my haunted house with all my memories, all my old aches, these basement trophies and baby clothes. I am moving in; and moving into a house once haunted is no quick task. It takes time, long moments melting into weeks.

Moving into myself will take years.

In the meantime, I take slow steps: gathering boxes, painting the dining room, building the furniture. I leave promises to my haunting, whispered in dark rooms, spoken into dank and dirty walls. *I will occupy. It is only you and me. At the end of it all, we only have each other.*

I will survive, not despite, but because. I will learn to love my haunting because it is mine.

I plant flowers among the rotten, splintered fence, ancient boards sprouting from the earth like bared teeth. I rebury the corpses that overturn soil in the garden. I clean the dust off the old mirrors, ignoring the things I see in the reflections. I sweep the creaky, tired floorboards. I yank ivy from the doors and windows. I let the light in. I peel back the old wallpaper, and I paint over the hollowed house. We mend together, my haunting and I.

A haunted house is hungry, so I offer it life.

* * *

I live within my body now, but I am still learning how to occupy it. One day my body will feel like a space I am allowed to live in.

Someday, my skin will fit. Not stretched too tight over the contents of my body, not sagging over my shoulders like an ill-fitting sweater.

I want to move past wanting. I want to become. Part of me itches — like all cramped things, my soul has always wanted expansion. My body cannot contain me for long, and I grow all the more impatient. I contain too much to be packaged into boxes.

I want to tear the scabs back to witness the new growth of flesh over once exposed bone. I want proof, proof that I am becoming, that my body has not left me behind. These scabs remain as physical evidence that I have survived.

Itch connotes healing. I try not to scratch.

Time ticks slowly by. I pass the years by in this haunted house, but I do not become part of it. We teach each other how to be. In time, it will be mine. In time I will be mine, too.

The new parts of myself, the old parts of myself, the ones I'd forgotten. They all come together in my haunted house. Here, I will expand. This will be a safe place, to gather the new and carry the old, and become and become and become. I want to be manifest. I am so often small, stuffed into the range of my own bones and allowed nothing more. I want to exist, outside of me, in the world. In the meantime, I will turn this haunted house into a home. I will teach this corpse how to be my body, one worth inhabiting.

I tell my haunted house, *even you can be loved.*

keloid scar

The original version of this piece was written in 2021.

is this all that love is?
    the birth of a haunting,
    the conception of a ghost.
    in the chambers of my heart, the hallways of my mind,
    you still walk,
    spectral punishment, forgive me.
    my heart still knows you linger here.
    these feelings cannot fade,
    as you echo in the cavernous halls of my mind,
    have I done something wrong?
    I loved you with my whole heart.
    in believing that you meant everything you said,
    was I foolish?
    was I deluded in thinking we could ever be?
    that it could ever be different?
    is this all there is?
    is this all that love is, just a keloid scar?
    have you left me with deeper wounds?

now i become an effigy

you loved me once, didn't you?
    tell me you loved me.
    tell me
    that it was real —
    that we were real.
    I am only ever seeing ghosts these days,
    so promise me that I am not just mistaking shadows.
    promise me I'm not remembering it wrong.
    promise me one version of you once wanted me.
    tell me it again,
    then light me up,
    cover me in gasoline,
    burn me like an effigy.
    I am too tired to worship anymore.
    if I can no longer offer you devotion,
    if I can only offer you tears,
    then let me add fuel to your fire.
    you will always be the heart of my heart.
    let me burn for you, sweet wound.
    I am so tired, my love.

I am tired as I am scarred.
you have left me marked and bloody.
I retain you. You haunt me.
I am in pieces.
you will always be the heart of my heart.
kept me wanting,
left me aching.
one day I will dream without your echoes.
until then, I will only burn and burn.

how the tide changes

I don't understand love. At the very least, I don't understand how to write about it. Love stretches the seams of our world and threatens to split the planet in two. I cannot begin to offer it any words or do it any justice. Perhaps love was never truly mine.

What can I write about love that has not already been written?
　Still.

Still, this is the sort of love that lingers. You hang like a perfumed haze on my heart, drifting in on cloudy nights. Your memory illuminated best in candlelight. Even well past an ending, even well past *moving on,* even still —
　Even still, I want.

Perhaps it's the unknowns that twist on my heartstrings. So much time has passed, but on nights like this I still crave you, my favored addiction. My stitched heart still seeks your claws. It hungers for a pain only you procure. Still — depict me in misery, lovely beast.
　Show me how even crimson blood comes in shades of blue.

* * *

I am lucky you left in the brighter months. Grief bleeds through the cracks in falling snow. Grey skies burst forth with magnetic pain, so I am thankful this frigid weather had not set in when you left. It is hard to remember to live when everything around you is dead. No blooms for months to come now — we can only have faith in the inevitable coming of spring. The cold persists, but I'm lucky the only evidence of you this winter is in memory.

Winter remembers you like flesh remembers favored lacerations. Wounds often reopen these days; fresh in winter as they ever were on those sticky, final days of summer. August saw the last of us, but it took well until November before I felt like I could breathe again at the mention of your name; poison-sweet.

Summer held me gentle and kissed my lips when you could not. I am lucky for August's gentle touch despite the pain. I found myself walking every night, trying to lose your memory in the thick, hot dusk. You kept following me home.
   I could never lose you in the darkness.

Still, I will always be grateful for August. It gave me more than I could've ever asked for. She was gentle to me in spite of everything, in spite of you. August breathed new life into my lungs even as I dug myself fresh graves.

For months, I practiced the act of release. I took laps around the pond at midnight. I taught myself to cry until I turned liquid. I froze myself solid. The memories of you came rushing back again; I spilled. Loving you proved my faith false until I built myself from scratch again.

Still, you worm your way through the cracks. Perhaps grief is never so linear. August saw the last of us, but you often hang around. You shattered me, but I still ache for you on nights like this. I cannot begin to piece together why; what about you makes you linger like this, the thought I just can't rid myself of, my summer storm, my perennial haunting, my hungry ghost. How I still want you, how I still crave you, my unforgiving spectral memory, my skeletal bloom.

Stitch me. Sew yourself into me. I will continue to cut you out. On the worst days, you fester like a wound. On the best, I retain the memory of you like a miserable scar.

Of course, dearest, you're already long gone. You're only an echo of an echo. Just a breath hanging in the air. I desire you best in my empty hours. You'll never be a remedy, despite the way I still pick at these scabs.

Only the bruised heart craves a ghost. You leech into me like poison memory.

Still, love, wounds like you take time to heal. Perhaps I like to see it, that old lesion; crimson reminder of love that once occupied this body. A reminder I ever loved at all.

**

Do not mistake my words — I offer you no fabric of my heart to hide yourself in. You are no longer allowed to witness me; I remain only ever yours in memory. See me only behind closed eyes, picture me only in dreams. It seems only fair, as sleep has never allowed me the sweet release of hiding from you. You always come wandering back, starving street cat scratching at the door.

Truly, darling, I am sick of thinking about you. I am exhausted of the way you pass through my mind like you own it; only spectral. No footprints left behind, a ghost dancing through these halls. No more than a memory, only a cool echo of what once was. My heart learns to ache over an imagined scent hanging in the air. My body learns to desire a reflection.

What is there to miss? Only an idea. Perhaps I only ever really loved the idea of you. After all, loving a picture of you was always easier than loving the person it depicted.

Love bears nostalgia, or perhaps, nostalgia bears love. They come intertwined, and the haze of summer left behind hangs on me like a stale perfume on this winter night.

Between us, there is nothing left. You remain only in memory. Perhaps the only thing that ever bridged the gap between us was our words. We fed into each other, great Ouroboros.

I still think of you in those days, far away, and I think of our little world we created. We bridged the gap between us. Yours became *ours*. We melted together in the heat, limbs sticky with summer sweat. I lost track of where I began and you ended.

You became all of my beginnings and endings, for a little while.

I still inhabit your New York summer, stone and concrete

trapping rising humidity. I imagined you in artist's vision. My muse. It's that summer that I carry within me tonight. New York summers swallow you up, I've found; perhaps that's what you channeled. Summers like that tend to crawl inside your throat and lay eggs. You seemed to have a similar effect. I wanted closeness, proximity, craving despite that sticky heat and always falling deeper. I trusted you, so I succumbed to madness for you, my sweet summer bloom.

You grew on me. I flowered for you, teaching you the quick paths to the central ventricle.

Let me be lost, if it only be within you. I knew that if I were lost inside, you would find me again. Pull me out. Steady my heart. Consume me.

Teach me how to live inside your skin as if it is my own.

That summer kept me addicted. Despite the distance, your presence hung in the very air. Like that New York humidity breathed within my bones, too. All-consuming heat, the kind that creeps in the pores of your skin and finds foothold perched beneath your chin. I felt you, too, building within me, something real, literal, tangible, and despite my habit of self-protection, my heart so carefully guarded —
   I wanted. I fell.

Safety be damned. Let the grand walls fall. Let us recreate Troy.

I caved to imagination like a hurricane. You were never more than a tropical storm; swallowed me up and left me in ruins.

When my heart felt like a flash flood, I sought higher ground in the refuge of your collarbone. There always was a beauty to that part of you, that destruction. I suppose I've always sought pain at the hands of another.

And like a flash of lightning, a thunderclap, you faded. Easy come, not so easy lost. You swayed into my life with a dancer's melody, addicting in every facet of your being, and how I craved. Oh, how I wanted. I had never felt such hunger before. You overtook my mind. Love like that poisons the air like a virus, infecting even within the deepest guarded bones.

You, my eternal monsoon; show me how the tide changes. I'll admit, I would always follow you into those watery depths.
Show me, my best-loved siren, how even sailors drown.

**

I opened myself up to your love, exposed my heart to you. You counted the beats, quickened for your observation. My gentle heart, shaky breaths, all surrendered to you. I have always been delicate and afraid of it.

Even now, I remain sugar-glass under your spectral hands.

My unforgivable heart, how I hate it for loving you so. Heartbreak cannot forgive a surrender so entire. I let the tide swallow me up. I let you crawl inside and rearrange things as you pleased, satisfied if it meant only bearing a mark of your memory.

Love like that leaves marks. Not always kiss-bruises, more cuts that leave scars. You were always sharp. I am not sure how I didn't see it coming. Perhaps I only ever wanted to be hurt. I handed you the blade, pointed square above my breastbone. *Carve me, here.*

I forgot to say the last part. I always seem to speak in half-finished sentences. I missed the most important words. *Carve me, here. Just be gentle to what you find underneath.*

Be gentle with it all: my keloid-scar heart, my fragile bluebird bones, my paper-thin lungs, so easily torn.

I am offering you surrender, so be gentle with it all, for it is far too easy for you to break me in two.

***

It's funny, you know. This habit I thought I'd broken long ago, an addiction, predisposed. I've been longing to kick it, haven't I? You're only a successor in a long line, but you cut so easily through skin and made your way to bone.

A child who learned to love pain seems to seek the blade even in adulthood, it seems, and love cuts deeper than any Swiss army knife ever could.

Sweet sacrament, show me how to turn my heart into a wrist.

I still admire the beauty of your marks. I'm not so sure I ever told you, but you cut with an artist's hand, my love. Perhaps that's why I still desire you. I favor the idea of being your muse in blood. Maybe that's why I let you in. I've always liked the look of scars.

The unfortunate fact is that I could not stop myself, even today, despite the way you carved me so profound. The locks keep changing themselves back, so I hope you've lost the key. Don't come in, for I would still surrender to your blade again and again.

Let me show you how time loops begin, darling. *Let me show you how time loops begin. Let me show you how time loops begin. Let me show you how time loops begin.*

* * *

Doe-eyes, cupid lips, your laugh, all honey-drip and twinkling stars. You always left me spilling. I've become a well of your memory, still sticky with expired love. You have left me wanting, occupied by your ghost breath.

At the end of it all, I suppose I got what I wanted. I bear the mark of your reciprocation. Though most days, it looks more like a gash.

You called me your *sharp little thing.* It still echoes inside.
  Turn my chest into a hollow drum and see what sound I make.

Here, there is no warm bed left for you. You have long since left. No bridge remains between our bodies. We have returned to our sides of this vast land. The dawn has come; our day is long since done. Let me tell you how even cathedrals collapse.
  Show me how even Rome fell.

I have not kept a space in my heart for you, but the path to forgiveness is long and winding. Healing, for me, was never so linear. August and November and February folded up against each other like origami wings. Expand, contract. Expand, expand, expand.

Expand. I open myself up for you again. Spread wide like fractured ribs. Show me love, remind me how you always liked to cut and slice your way through bone.

Do not mistake my intentions — I am an open door you are not allowed through.

Grief like this has hills and valleys, darling. Dips and spikes so sharp they pierce me through. Old wounds always open on nights like this. Winter always leaves my skin dry, so it's no surprise these cuts split open again. I always find myself picking at the scabs in absentminded memory.

Show me how best to bandage a cut that never congeals. The flow of blood never seems to cease. I keep soaking through the fabric.

Show me how scalded skin remembers. Remind me how heat blisters become scars. I will put my hand to the stove again if you only ask.

Still, I seek forgiveness, forgiveness for loving you and crawling under your knife. A willing offering, if only for one more glance. One more sweet kiss, my executioner, and I will bleed for you. Touch me again, just once, and I will hack myself in two.

Show me how the dagger depicts devotion. Show me how even the lamb can love the blade.

I am in search of a peace from you, a sense of finality. One day, I will think of you for the last time. One day, you will be nothing more than a shadow on the horizon.

Despite that, tonight, you still occupy my thoughts. I don't give myself the tender care that would permit healing. These stitches continue to itch. I keep picking at the same old scabs.

Perhaps that's for the best.

After all, I always thought I looked better as a wound than a man.

* * *

Nights like this, I wonder if you ever think of me. Perhaps, I am nothing more than a moment. A faraway glance cast backwards into summer. A heartbeat in the grander scale of your life. It makes a certain sense to me — you were always my ghost, but I was never yours.

Still, I remember your words darling, carved in deep, how you believed you would never find another like me. How you never wanted to let me go. (At the end, you apologized for making promises you couldn't keep. Never say never, I suppose.)

Remind me how even the most honest truths become lies. Come on, love. Show me how the tide changes.

* * *

In the grand scheme, I never fit. Never quite found my place. We were not meant to be; not star-crossed, no path paved for us. No red string linking our earthly bodies. Fate never cast a glance upon us. I have long since accepted that we were never written in the stars.

The only story written for us is etched in history's halls. I will keep records of it, the brief history of us, our minute and hungry affair. This is the book of love, long since closed, cover bound and sewn shut with tattered thread.

In the halls of history, all great loves look just the same. History has no remarks for us. In time, even we will become a blur.

I admit you left me consumed — I let it happen. Saw an unhinged jaw and climbed right in, like passing through a window. I hoped there was a future for us on the other side of your mouth. I have always mistaken love for consumption. I have a prey urge.

Whatever it is that you hold – you *held* – over me, I don't believe I'll ever understand it. I have decided to stop trying. You are no longer my muse, and I am tired of bleeding.

Sweet one, you will never be a whole heart. I carry you in fragments, and although they remain often sharp, I will no longer pierce myself with your memory. I wish you the best, beloved haunting. The addiction to the pain you procure is poisoning me, and it is time to let go. I send you, onto the next plane, a place I cannot yet go in life. Tonight, I send you into the hereafter. Show me how even the most marred heart manages to heal. Show me how even ghosts let go.

I release you, now.
   Farewell.

wood music

The original version of this poem was written in 2018.

listen carefully
   to how
   the wind pauses in the forest,
   hesitating,
   when his fingers tremble the strings
   delicately,
   breath of angels,
   tender promise
   the world's on pause
   when
   his slender hands
   trace the strings
   musician's devotion,
   the empty air carries that melody.
   it sounds something like love
   and it sounds something like youth
   long lost.

a deity of some kind

The tears well up, spilling like shattered glass.
　I do not know how I will continue.
　A deity of some kind cradles my cheeks, telling me there is only one thing left to do.
　Put it to page.
　I tell her I am tired. My heart is weary.
　I have fought for so long. I am so weak.
　She tells me to weave my exhaustion into words.
　I tell her that I do not yet know how to convert these sorrows into something beautiful.
　She tells me that I have already done so,
　For living despite is beauty enough.
　The only thing left to do is to put them down.
　I let her holy voice speak through me; I put pen to paper.
　I stitch sorrow into language and spin a fabric of creation.

the angel of creation manifests

I understand the present as some kind of awakening.

A force swallows me up. My skull aches, near to splitting. Hand reaches for the pen in darkness, and I scrawl a few words on a page. It's only momentary satiation. I feel propelled to create, imbued both with earthly desire and divine desperation. An inspiration. An all-consuming hunger.

Religious awakening? Angel of creation? I do feel inspired, lifted up on something with wings. Prophesying without intervention, channeling creation self-contained. I am fit to burst. Splitting at the seams. Something glows inside me, abstract and limitless, powerful and overwhelming. A tidal wave creeping in a dream. There is a beauty and a terror to it.

I have always believed holiness to be the sort of force that exists beyond human bounds. Angels never manifest inside the body itself. A vision or a specter, but the body remains singular. I had never considered the possibility of divine possession.

Still, this feeling has the texture of holiness to it - metallic spoon taste and body-burning brightness. I cannot attribute it to an exterior force. No moon controls these tides. I am anchored only in myself. I sink only as a result of my own intervention.

No angels in occupancy. Only one inside this body.

Whatever is happening inside me is contained solely within me, in these halls of muscle and bone. Traced on neural paths alone. What my heart knows is only mine.

Does divine intervention have some sort of sensation to it? Awakenings have a weight to them.

I am both the glass and the light and the crosswalk. I am the refraction and the image projected. I am both myself and my reflection and the idea of me carried in others.

Maybe these things were never meant to be contained to one person. Perhaps my foundations are too shaky to contain an awakening. I have always thought myself weak. Still, I am captured in stasis and yet propelled with constant transformation.

I used to believe I would feel some presence of rebirth within me when it happened. The gears turning, the walls shifting. The great movement of the universal fabric contained inside. Perhaps some evidence of change.

Yet, whatever I am undergoing now is a process unbeknownst to me. I cannot see the strings. I pilot the ship and yet do not control its course, no knowledge of path or destination.

Bludgeoned over the head and woke up new. I'm still in total darkness, groping for the light switch on stucco walls. Pitch-black revelation. Maybe I'm still waking up.

I cannot begin to picture an end to this. I know there is a finality to it, because a state like this could never promise permanence. Without an end, the light inside me will one day burn me out. I am bearing witness to something holy, a full-body possession, breath of creation that spreads throughout me like a virus or a weed.

I wonder if my physical body could ever be enough to contain my spirit. I feel vast and expanseless, fit with enough feeling for at least one other. I am too much for this thin skin. I am not so sure if it is holy inspiration, creative drive, or simply madness. Either way, this is all mine, only mine, and all contained within me.

The only release is within the margins of a page, where I can hope to write something that matters, something that reaches in and pulls out a truth I am yet still struggling to discover. Rearranging my guts and seeking meaning in blood droplets like tea leaves. Searching for answers in hope the words reveal themselves to me before I know them. I am hoping, in the margins, that I can find an explanation for it all, a common understanding, clarity in this divine undertaking.

There is an unearthly beauty to all of this. It leaves me self-possessed, propelled by a spirit that feels entirely my own yet wholly unfamiliar. Myself and yet not me at all.

* * *

Lately, I am beginning to see through the cracks, looking through the great gap into the divine plan. Whatever cracks I'm seeing through, I'm not sure. I cannot begin to make out the image beyond the doorway. Awakening, punishment, blessing, possession.

I am beginning to wonder if this feeling can be solved in the search for religion, but I'm more convinced to bring any more gods into this mix than the ones already tangled up inside me would be a great inconvenience for everyone involved. God complicates. Religion seeks to simplify. I wish not to surrender my complexities and contradictions to the hands of the omnipotent.

I have decided to search for the answers myself, to bite down on the bullet and stare into the sun. I can only hope that as I bear witness, I will not be consumed wholly within the fire I tend inside myself, Roman hearth, the very living fire of the city within. I am set alight. The body and the home and the city and the heart, all on fire. In Greek, it's *kardia* — the very same word for heart. Heart, flame, scorched earth. I am coming apart from the force of my own being. The flames inside me are inconsolable, this fire unrelenting. It climbs and swells, crackling hands and unforgiving heat, asking both to swallow and consume, to expand and illuminate. I am left only to bear witness.

For now, I am just letting it be. I surrender to the great tide, even if that means drowning. I let myself see through the cracks, at the glinting light, into something else. The future, perhaps, or enlightenment, maybe. It feels revelatory, holy, especially in the striking fear and overwhelming burden of it all.

The words, I find, come easiest in the moments where I let myself go. If I keep my body occupied, my hands busy, but I let my mind drift, the feeling inside me will begin to swell, to stretch and breathe, threatening to burst, to take me with it.

I am hoping to salvage what I can before the rupture.

I've begun to take notice of things I haven't before. In the shower, my veins run electric, cast in illumined blue, hard-candy vibrancy. They have never looked so bright before. I am stilled by it, breath sucked from my lungs. I was not aware my body could contain a color so vibrant. Universe, cosmos, galaxy, all contained within a single vein.

It has no meaning. It is simply there, that blue; that vibrancy. It is asking nothing, offering only life. The body persists. I exist with or without my consent.

My consciousness feels small within the vastness of my own body. I am bearing witness to a becoming I cannot remember beginning. I am splitting at the seams and leaking light.

* * *

I recall a figure drawing course, not all that long ago, and how I learned to memorize the human body through smudged charcoal. The figures came to life in slow strokes under my blackened fingertips.

Half the time, it was like it came to life without me noticing. One moment, it was charcoal on newsprint, but eventually, the rough outlines would form. A body would begin to take shape, a person realized in black and white, without my knowledge of its undertaking. I was only an instrument in the process of creation, only a channel spoken through.

I am coming to understand creative undertaking as a prophetic act.

I am beginning, for the first time I think, to etch out the bounds of the person I consider myself to be. At first, this seems an easy task — I live within my own mind, and I move within my own body, after all. I inhabit myself, so I should know myself.

However, I am learning I know myself only in partial fragments. I am trying to bridge the gap between seen and witnessed and realized in newsprint. The body that occupies the world is not the same that my eyes see, not the same that my hands etch in charcoal; on paper flesh. My conception of self is refracted through a million lenses until it is entirely unrecognizable.

The only solution seems to be seeking simplicity. I am working only to realize the big picture, the grand structural gestures of where my mind meets my soul and my body meets the world around me.

It is easier to realize the negative space than it is to represent myself within it. In sketching myself, I favor the simple knowledge, the absolute knowns: the color of my eyes, the length and width of my feet, the scars on the back of my hands.

Absolutes. The dictionary definition of me outlined only by the body's edges. Material presence in the material world. The simple reminder I exist, that I am physical. I hope this will be enough of an anchor.

My mind is undergoing revelation beyond me, so I rely on my body as proof I exist at all.

I am taking notice of electric blue illuminated in dorm bathroom light, in the way my skin seems more a filter than a solid. See-through, like there's no person, only veins. No body, only color. More an idea than a construction. My consciousness and my body inhabit two separate footholds in the cosmic theatre. I am spliced into layers, becoming less and less comprehensible until I am no more than an abstracted frame; Kandinsky composition.

It keeps shifting, keeps changing. I can see now, the parts I've missed, the parts lacking in the original sketch. The whole picture has changed, despite the sameness of the figure.

I am not sure if I know myself at all.

the author's field-guide to resilience

These days, I leak pain through my pores like open wounds.

These days, it's all the same mantra: *I will continue to try my best. I will continue to survive.*

I tell myself it has to come out somewhere, learnt through the heart and expelled through material flesh. I bleed colors too pale for the naked eye to see.

Nonetheless, I feel ever the more empty. The in-between moments feel like miniature eternities, microcosmic forevers. They expand inside me with promised ache, despite my best attempts at resilience. Yet, I have a penchance for reckless optimism, fueled by the hope that in time, I will find myself on the other side of all of this. Heart willing, I will survive all of this. Spirit willing, I will make it through.

I can survive all of this. All of this pain, this jagged and bleeding present time. I can survive all of this, this wounded self I occupy, this exhausted body I drag with me, these unsteady footholds I rely on.

I will survive it, this world in which I am allowed to exist yet not inhabit.

I am filtered through the glass, fragmented and abstracted light beam. Kaleidoscopic depiction of self. Nothing is absolute. Shattered, splintered. I ache through every moment. I ache in this moment. All of these moments, collecting like raindrops, bearing down under impossible weight. I am trying not to crack under the pressure.

I make this a mantra. I will live in spite of myself, and survive in spite of everything else.

* * *

I am waiting on the platform for a train that never comes. Even when I can hear it creeping close, coming in the distance, tried tracks squealing metal screams, the sound fades again, no more than a memory. No more than a prayer, perhaps. Perhaps it never existed at all. Perhaps I was so hopeful that my mind conceived it. Imagination to placate the weary soul.

Every night, I dream of approaching trains.

Sometimes, earnest hope betrays. I am trying to keep faith that hope will come through, eventually. Hope carried on angels' wings.

Even today, the clock counts down, minutes, neon promised arrival. It gets closer and closer, but the train never comes. The morning never dawns. I am in stasis. I am stagnant. I am still.

Frozen in time. Trapped in the gaps. Known only to myself and the in-betweens.

Lately, I am needle-pricked and broken bare. Stripped raw and exposed. I ache and pray to be known, rather than simply memorized. Most people that try make little more than half-hearted attempts. Others don't even begin to pretend.

I ache to be seen in entirety, to be known, rather than committed to memory in fragments. I am a person, but I am making myself a prayer. I become a saint in half-bodies. People expect this to be enough. I am existing in partial selves. I resign myself to half-felt truths and half-lived lives, always searching for the catharsis in the in-betweens; a semblance of peace wherever I can find a moment to breathe. It is a desperate stab towards life. Base Instinct. Raw desire.

I am breathing in screams, bearing wounds. Every day, another needle, new stitch. Wounds opened over barely-scars. Scabbed and wearing past worn. I am so often threadbare.

Yet, I am desperate to survive, even if on raw human instinct alone. I've made survival a habit, a practice to continually embody. Survival as my singular religion.

I'll admit, it becomes harder and harder to have faith – in survival, in myself. My own strength wavers. The self requires an external space to occupy. I have no place outside these walls. Most days, I inhabit a world only within skin and bone.

On my weakest days, I let muscle memory carry me through. My body has always known how to survive better than my mind. I let my cells do the work. Even stretched thin and torn through, my heart never ceases, my lungs continue to expand and contract, cycling breaths.

My body persists even when I cannot.

I am reserving pain for the moments in-between, offering myself little time to feel for fear of imminent collapse. There is no space for the screams to release, no expanse of woods wide enough, no pit deep enough to bear them, so I swallow them. I transform poison into essential nutrients. I teach my lungs to breathe sour air.

The human body can survive past hope; I persist on life alone. Human nature. Survival, a habit best learned with constant practice. I rely on mantras and prayers. *I have survived worse, and I will survive through worse.*

Yet, the little voice always begins to doubt (and this is its' fundamental job, to echo fear and resound throughout the body)—*is this all there ever is?*

My father tells me I will never reach the finish line. He promises me that this is all there ever is, and all that there ever will be. Why should I try, if I will always live half-truths and inhabit in-betweens? He's convinced my fractures will always show. He's convinced I will never be truly whole as I so desire. Incomplete construction. I will always be a half-finished sketch only resembling a man.

He tells me that I will always be two-way glass. Everyone will see into me, but I will see nothing outside myself, occupying a room alone with my aches and my pains. Just me and the glass. Seen through yet never looking out.

The little voice inside me often believes him (this, too, is its' job, to absorb cruel words and repeat them in perpetuity) — if the future is already planned and painted out, then what is the point of switching mediums?

He wants me to give up, but he doesn't know it. The Instinct. He can't feel it, etched into my bones, the very fibers of my being entire, known by every cell, little vessels hellbent on survival. My body works so hard to survive. It heals where I cannot begin to. My body knows the path when my heart gets lost. It leads me home even with closed eyes, even in total darkness.

My body persists in spite of me, so I will live in spite of myself, and survive in spite of everything else.

* * *

The world is a door still closed to me. I leave claw marks against the wood but I never manage to make it through. I do not even make a dent. In this not-yet-world, I cannot begin to exist — condemned to occupy a universe that isn't entirely my own.

In my not-world, I settle for record-keeping. I become a recordist of my own pain. I am the author of the field-guide to survival in the impossible age.

I am still trying to turn the desperation for survival into resilience. Yet, most days I am only recording pain, cataloguing moments with the dedication of a devoted librarian. Tracing scars in scrap paper — *record-keeping for a wholer body.* Record-keeping for when the present eventually becomes the past.

I am leaving notes for myself. *Once, this was all I was. But can't you see, now, that we made it?*

My best-held hopes are that this will all be in the past someday. I am all stitches and staples now, but one day I will inhabit a skin that fits. *Our skin will be our own. Our body fully occupied. No more hiding. No more half-truths. Our world: ours entire.*

My future self leaves promises for me to find. *I told you so. I told you one day that we would make it.*

But today, I am forcing the emptiness to be enough, committing the pits in my stomach and pockmarks in my heart to memory in the meantime. *One day*, my cells remind me, *this will be no more than a story to tell.* My body knows hope like marrow.

It's half instinct and half desperation. The self that succumbs is a self that sinks, committing instead to corpsehood, digging graves in broad daylight. I hold myself up. My body has impossible weight, but still, I carry myself. I bear the burden. I will make the impossible bearable, somehow.

I remind myself: *you won't know how to do it until the doing gets done.*

Those who have walked this path before me have managed, and they have managed worse. My half-lives have been quarter-lives for others. Partial existences - contained, no escape in sight. No world to occupy. Others never managed to breach the surface, pretend-living whilst drowning inside themselves.

I *will* breach the surface. I will break free. I will be whole.

So I continue stitching myself together. Again and again. I weave myself into a tapestry with borrowed yarn. The world will wear holes in me, but I will keep stitching. I will manage. I will persist within my impossibilities.

Life cannot simply just be holding on. I tell myself - half prayer, half promise - *this cannot be all there is. Life is not a waiting room.*

Every morning, I wake up overgrown. I begin new dawns by peeling off the extraneous layers, cutting off the excess. I hack and twist my body into a body capable of survival, a self capable of making it through. I shape myself and I force myself through existence. I will make it through.

I will make it through: this is an order. This is a prayer. This is threadbare, worn-down existence, stripped raw to the fibers of human desperation alone. And I will survive in spite of it all. I will live past the impossible.

As I repair myself, I stitch the words into my flesh. I will live in spite of myself, and survive in spite of everything else.

* * *

I am always learning how to wear pain like a second skin. I am a relentless optimist, boring my fingers into hope until it breaks free, offers solace. Claw through deep earth until light shows. I keep finding ways out, no matter how deep I'm buried.

I drag myself forward for a self I picture that one day will exist. Still, I doubt, not so sure that self will ever come to be. Perhaps it's only hope. Perhaps I'm only fortune-telling. Perhaps I'm only praying. I suppose I can never know, so I hold onto hope.

Today, I hope that it is more than desperation. Tomorrow, I will hope the same.

Nonetheless, I find present joy in half-lived lives. I breathe screams and bend them into a shape that resembles optimism. I'm depending on self-contained creation until hope comes through. I imagine Christ started with the in-betweens and went from there.

When I cannot create myself, I will create other things. I will paint myself on these pages. If I am bleeding, then I will use the blood as ink. I will write poems on flayed skin. I will carve the mantras into my bones. I will persist. I will survive. I will make it through.

I will etch beautiful things into existence, bandage my sores, and lick my wounds. If this world cannot be wholly mine, then I will decorate the spaces I am permitted to inhabit. I will make the darkest and dankest rooms into palaces and gallery spaces. Wherever I am allowed, I will make it beautiful. It's the only thing I know how to do. Maybe it's the only thing left.

My world is small, and my body is bruised and broken. Nonetheless, I will make it vibrant in spirit and nature. I let my pain water vibrant gardens of my own construction. I will paint my in-betweens in bright shades rather than gray hues. Fuchsia, crimson, violet. I rely on the simple and minute beauty that I am allowed.

Just the act of putting a floral Bandaid on the deepest wound is enough to begin to repair. I will infuse beauty into all the ugly things. I will teach myself to laugh, even speared through. I stitch myself together with sheer determination and raw fibers of creation alone. I will make my world beautiful, even if that's all I can do.

Perhaps that's all that resilience is — learning to manage with what remains. I continue to persist and continue to create. I paint the world in bruised and bloody colors. I transform bodily pain into worldly beauty.

An abridged definition of the entirety of human determination: to do everything you can to survive and to paint the world radiant with whatever is left behind.

Even if it's simply skin and bone.

II

Part Two

brother by the interstate

brother, tell me,
    was your sacrifice worth it?
    you washed it all away,
    the holy impurity you carried so long cleansed at last.
    brother,
    I hope it's alright.
    I buried you in a pine box,
    in a clearing off of the interstate.
    when it all was said and done,
    I lay by the fresh mound of loose dirt,
    grass tickling against scar-etched skin
    looking up at the stars.

brother, do you remember?
    when you were young,
    you'd point out the constellations to me.
    you always knew all their names
    and all their stories.
    you always knew those sort of things.
    your heart was always better than mine.
    I wish you could've stayed soft.

I have always had to be sharp.

brother, forgive me.
    there is six feet of earth separating us now,
    so do forgive my cynicism,
    despite the cross
    marking the place you will spend eternity,
    constructed by calloused hand
    near the place you now lay —
    despite the loyalty and persistence of your faith
    God never came to save you.
    — and yet, it's not the first time
    either of us believed in a hero
    who always failed to deliver,
    is it?

brother,
    I never meant for you to be the sacrificial lamb.
    I never meant for you to feel impure.
    brother,
    your impurity was always holy,
    unlike mine.

brother,
    you never had a choice.
    from birth, you were always cursed.
    you never took it to heart.
    I wish I could say the same for myself.

brother,
    I wish I could tell you now,

that against any number of curses,
for any price,
heaven and hell be damned,
I'll always carry you.

brother,
for how long have we been trading lives?

brother,
how can I tell you,
I forgive you for it all?

the sister

The original version of this poem was written in 2019.

your sister once whispered your name
    even in these times
    you can still hear her speak it in ghost breaths.
    it was she who carried you
    Home
    and
    it was she who taught you
    the importance of your name spoken softly
    by someone you love.
    she peeled oranges
    she brushed your dirty, knotted hair.
    she wiped away the tears
    for the first time in a long time
    a meal was not a question
    but a constant
    and love was,
    too.

the heart is a scared animal

you saw my weaknesses,
    the soft underbelly of the scared creature beneath me,
    and I handed you the knife,
    offering — *begging*,
    pierce me. only gently.
    open me up,
    just enough to get through. *cut into me. come in.*

wax + wane

the story begins like this.
    the door of the past slams shut,
    leaves us confined to the halls of memory alone.
    one is always left to beg
    for the touch of wanting spirit hands,
    aren't they?
    one is left to ache for spectral love.
    I wax and wane for you still, my love,
    sacred ghost,
    shell of my body still yours,
    occupied by haunted desire,
    marked by phantom bodies.

sanctified

Kneeling before you, I ask you again,
    Let me be your gun, let me be your knife,
    Let me be your hands, your arms, your beating heart –
    Let me be your sacrifice.
    Let nothing separate us ever again,
    If I am ever to be torn
    – or worse, to drift away from you
    Let you be the last thing my eyes see.
    Imprint yourself behind my eyelids,
    brand yourself upon my flesh,
    Allow me the assurance that I'll never exist as one being again.
    Tell me it again,
    Say my name.
    Carbon lifeforms be damned,
    tell me that we are more than entities.
    Existing separately, tell me that we're conjoined.
    Melded.
    Souls imprinted with the same marks of *belonging*,
    Mirror forms, enduring permanence
    Remind me that no cell,
    no continent,
    no amount of distance,

no length of time,
could separate us again. Tell me it again.
Burn it into my flesh with the iron of your look, carve it into my bones with the scalpel of your touch, carve it into my soul in the language of your lips, I am begging you –
Brand me. Mark me.
The sizzling sound of burning flesh, the stinging, burning, *ecstatic* feeling, and when my flesh no longer maintains the mark of you then carve it into my bones.
If it is not permanent enough,
then take a razor to my chest and etch me in crimson rivulets,
Scar me with your memory, lest I forget.
Sacrifice me. I will martyr for you.
Gut me. Tear me, devour me with your wolf teeth,
Your tongue bloody, my flesh hanging from your canines,
I want to be your worthy sacrifice,
your promised victim,
in any lifetime, there no death more just,
more *sanctified*,
then that at the edge of your blade,
Not murder, never simply violence –
violence as an appendage of ecstasy, of attraction.
Desire me. Desire me as a god desires
a virgin slaughtered,
Desire me as your lamb of sacrifice,
I will remain, your disciple,
Kneeling at your feet, at the altar of your body –
And there is no mistaking you for Christ.
The wounds on your wrists confirm it.

ritual of the butcher & the lamb

his fingers trace the paths of your scars,
    calloused hand guided by your wrist.
    tightened grasp, breath catching in your throat,
    heart beating like hummingbird wings.
    you have never had to speak for him to understand.
    this is your private language,
    spoken in glances,
    channeled in electric, hungry touch.
    he hears you just the same
    this is where you split me open,
    this is where you marked yourself on me,
    turned me into a holy relic of your ardor.
    it remembers you, just as I remember you, just as I always will.
    in life you carved me, so my flesh will remember you unto death.
    the mind may forget, but the body remembers.
    my body remembers.
    my body knows now that your violence
    was always the echoes of your devotion.
    holy love resounding unto flesh and bone.

these days,
    his hands always return to your scars,

the expanse of his love charted in a straight line,
the distance between two points,
the space between himself and you,
mapped in scar tissue.
a love letter, in his own way.
carve me, here.
show me that this body is more than just mine.
of course, he'd neglected to mention
that killing you would have killed him too.
he was courting death as he carved into you,
in your death, I will consume you.
in my death, you will eventually consume me.
as I have consumed your mind,
ravaged your synapses and broken down your highest walls,
your sickness will overtake me.
I cannot live without you, but I cannot live with you.
I will kill you, and I will let you be the thing that kills me.
as the saw cut through bone, he was calling to death,
not just whispering to her,
but beckoning —
deciding your death and sealing his own fate
in the same breath.
it was your last supper, and he was preparing for his very own.
no less conjoined in death than in life,
his limbs only an extension of your own.

you look at him,
    eyes admitting that
    you'd rather he'd carved
    his name into your bones
    flesh decays, the only reminder to the living

of the inevitable.
of course, *he* was your inevitable — fate carved,
promised death, always at his hand.
death has no importance as long as he is near,
but if he had etched his name into your ribs,
there would no grave that could separate between your bodies.

the marks you retain,
    less a reminder that you belong,
    (although you surely do belong to him),
    but more a reminder,
    that the link between your bodies
    is more than just linked by Eros,
    by desire.
    but that his heart beats in your chest
    his breaths catch in your throat,
    your animal throat, his animal heart.
    always hungry creatures,
    tearing each other forever,
    even in death, you will not part.

you focus on his breaths,
    his breaths that bring you more life
    than your own.
    you crave to come together completely with him,
    lose the gaps and lose the definitions of
    self and single and individual,
    to be one, one, one. His.
    His mind in your mind, your heart in his heart,
    until the very day your flesh begins
    to peel off your bones,

maggots crawling in your insides
and eating you away,
until you are nothing,
nothing but bones bleached white in the sun.
His name would remain marked into your bones until you
– as a whole, not an individual –
crumble and disintegrate into dust.
until you are nothing
but dust among the particles of soil in the air.
Even then your bones will echo him,
his love.

resounding frequencies of your dual music,
    a century in the future,
    your song carved into the face of the earth
    as if by god's hand himself.
    even in a million years, he would still be the extension of you.
    it would take armies to bring you down,
    sieges to topple you.
    and even then,
    you'd return to the battlefield in his armor.
    you'd rather die in the bounds of his skin
    than anywhere near yours.

you seek to blur until the bounds between
    you and him are washed away,
    until he is within you,
    until he *is* you, until you are him,
    until they'd have to kill both of you to tear apart that bond –
    one deeper than mere flesh define.
    his body is nothing less than consecrated ground

and you worship until he is god, you are god,
until there is no god aside from the god that you found in him.
he tells you this:
the gods first created humans with 4 arms and 4 legs,
but those forms were too powerful,
enough to topple their reign and tear the skies down –
so Zeus took them — you, me, us — apart
splitting them — you, me, us — into two halves.
leaving us divided, searching for wholeness,
you tell him,
I have always been waiting to find you.

you are not just one individual; you are the holiest of forms.
    you have not just found your divinity.
    you have been scarred with it.
    discard old religion,
    your god carved himself into you with his own hand,
    consecrated your body with desire,
    red-hot and hungry.

and as you trace his scars, you repeat to him your pact –
    carved in flesh, in blood, in bone.
    let the only thing that kill me be you.
    otherwise, I will not die.
    I will climb from any grave to return to you, my flesh.
    my love shall rise me from the ground like Lazarus.

sparrow

the safest place is the sheltered world,
    no questioning eyes tucked inside.
    out there, you're naked.
    skin stripped bare, flayed raw
    grief peels you like an apple,
    leaving you vulnerable to every passing glance.
    out there, everyone's asking questions.
    where have you been?
    why are you crying?
    you cry through whole classes these days.
    your heart is ruptured earth.
    you're finding better and better ways to hide.
    they are always asking questions,
    and you can only manage the same four words.
    someone died. someone important.
    you can't bear something
    as simple and meaningless as French class.
    you can't read this language,
    every word materializing her name.
    when you try and read, her face flashes in your mind
    the professor is speaking but it drifts past your ears. airwaves.

you cry after dance rehearsal,
tucked on a bench in the corner to listen to her voice again,
her songbird melody.
you don't know how to reconcile
that everyone has learned to live without her — except you.
it all seems meaningless without her.
no explanation carries the pain that echoes inside you.
you're no more than a shell.
you are a hollowed robin's egg,
spirit of flight long since abandoned.
she was always so thin,
baby bird, so close to falling from the nest.
you never could have shielded her from predators.
in your skin you only see her these days.
you are shrinking, always thinner.
your heart is paper-thin and punctured through.
gentle sparrow, so close to passing but so close to flying.
in the end, she ended up snapping her own wings.

moonflower (bloom of love)

The original version of this piece was written in 2019.

I knew from the beginning that you would break my heart.

That was how we met — in a moment of swift heartbreak. You pierced me through, the twice-edged sword of ardor. Even still, I bloom red with love for you. Always and forever, for you.

I wonder what it would've been like if I had you for longer, here. You are as whole as you ever were, but it breaks my heart to know I will never know the way you moved throughout the world. Not truly. Not you, entire.

I am still learning how to reconcile with pieces of you. I am always holding onto these fractions of you; in music, in pictures, in words. You exist in this world in the fragments you left in everyone you loved and everyone who loved you. I hope this will be enough.

You will only ever be a memory, captured in a photograph. You etched yourself into the surface of this big, blue planet, and even the earth aches without your feet pressing into the soil. It took to swallowing you up with the hope of mending. You are underneath it, now.

You have always been the right person, but I met you at the wrong time. How could I miss you for so long? How long did I pass you before I knew you?

Did I miss important time? Can you ever forgive me for that?

Sometimes I am not sure I can forgive myself.

Tonight I seek not to talk about guilt. The ache for you will always remain a reminder that you existed. I will remain grateful for that pain, despite the sharpest edges. You reverberate on the halls of my heart. Love resounds in grief, valley echos.

These days, I know you best as the moon. (It seems a fitting title — you always did come out at night. The brightest things shine best in darkness, and even your memory seems lit in silver light.) On nights like this, where you hang highest in the sky, this is where I miss you the most. Tonight, my pale hands reach out for you through the great curtains of the cosmic stage. I hope you can feel it wherever you are, my love. I can always feel you.

You have never been entirely gone, still streaming through the windows and capturing me in your cool embrace. Your presence hangs around, my love. Even in empty rooms, you cradle my cheeks and kiss my tears dry.

Tonight I will write of the love that hides behind grief. Most times heartbreak is empty and lonely and cruel, but this heartbreak is like none I've known before. You remind me that heartbreak can be gentle, my moonsong. Heartbreak like yours leaves delicate scars, love tattooed in permanence, even past death. Grief is the reminder of how much you were, and still are, to me. I have learned even grief can be sugar-sweet when it echoes your name.

Loving you has never made me heavy. It has always made me light.

* * *

I spoke in many loves before I met you.

I sought once to avoid heartbreak. Despite those words passing through my lips, I knew that it was inevitable. I recognized you even then, sweet one.

In hundreds of languages of love do I recognize you.

But despite my fear, despite everything, I fell. I fell with no hesitations and no restrictions, without question. I never doubted that I would. For me you have always been everything in between, and that was love. Imperfect, broken, aching. I will always know you best by your imperfections and love you more for them. I have never been whole and despite the unknowing space between us, I know you love me just the same.

This is our sacred space, the place I imagine best for us. Blond hair turned silver in the cool glow. When you shine, we can swim all night in the vast pool of the cosmos. I follow you, far past the earth, further into your impossible realm. Not another soul in this shining vastness, I think. Only you and I, the sole inhabitants of this cosmic scene.

These are our private moments, between me and the moon. We drink back the slow tide of the Milky Way in gleaming cups. You guide me into a slow dance on this planetary stage, our sweet song resounding through star-strings. The universe resounds for you, rhythmic and regular. Familiar — this sound always hummed in your bones. Perhaps the universe was only ever calling you back.

Despite the beauty of these moments, I cannot stay with you forever. You will always have to go.

You guide me back on bright streams, shimmering rivers burnished in silver. As we walk, I remind myself not to be marred by the judgments of strangers when you are not around. We need not consider anyone else while the universe casts us in infinite light. I have always known some people don't understand my love. I tell myself they don't need to - this is our place. Only you and I should matter.

Still, when they speak your name with malice in their spit I shake, desperate to tear myself apart so they can see the illumined gold this love casts on my bones. Perhaps if I were to tear into myself, they could see all you are to me. Perhaps then they would understand.

This love is unfamiliar to them because that love is new. Our language of love does not speak for them. It is cosmic, and love like that is not so easily comprehended. It is strange, and oh god, in so many ways it is broken and aching. Perhaps they can only see the pain. But still, you make me whole. You put back all my broken pieces.

Other people, they wish to peel it apart and examine the strings, the psychology. the moments before and the moments after. Beginnings and endings and today. They don't begin to understand. I'm not so sure they are capable.

They have always thought you a droplet and I have always known you as an ocean.

If they read us truly, they would not need an explanation. They would only read love and nothing else. And although it breaks my heart that they cannot know you like I know you, that they will never understand, I pray to every god to ever exist that they might one day understand just a fraction of what you mean. What you always meant.

My love, your soul cast the world in silver light, and you are still just as luminous. The moon's beauty lingers in memory even when shrouded behind clouds.

* * *

When you left, even the sky wept for you. I remember that day while the snow fell and I sat down on a tiled floor, learning of news that alters my heart every moment —
   you were gone.

(I imagine the ferry was carrying you over the stars by then, towards the great hereafter.)

We all ached for you, even if we couldn't put our fingers on it. The world felt an absence of love. Your absence still resounds, turning the world into an empty room.

You will always linger, but my love, you were so much more before that splitting moment. The earth may have cracked and taken you, but you are still here. I don't have the answers and I do not know of a God above, but my faith rests knowing that the sun shines where you are, that you don't hurt anymore. That you and the gods beyond join hands.

I hope the stars are not so lonely. Perhaps that is where you were always meant to be, tucked in the great planetary fabric, wrapped in cosmic curtains. I always thought you fit best amongst the stars, my love.

I hope your heart is not so heavy anymore. Where you are, can you separate the hurt from the love? Even without you here, you make the darkness a little brighter.

I know we never joined hands, and I never stared into your eyes. But despite the regrets, the sins, the sadness, I know that I have someone to love who loves me. Your light reflects on me, even now. I remain forever illumined in the silver glow of the moon.

Despite my pain, I do not regret a single part of you. Time did not waste herself on you. Even your brief moment was enough. You made more of barely thirty years than many do in a hundred.

By the winding path of grief, your memory remains.

I know when the gods brought you back, they brought you back tender and gentle. They crafted you with care and they took you back with kindness, embracing your skin and bones and your brown eyes. Embracing your big heart, overflowing with sadness. Your honey-sweet words. Your amber voice, always so lit in grief. They always loved you, so I know they welcomed you home with open arms, whispering sweet words in your ears. I imagine they were as delicate to you as you are to me.

I hope now that you can rest, no longer heavy. I hope they mended your broken parts as you have always mended mine.

I still struggle, knowing the presence of thousands and thousands of lost moments. I think about how there could have been an infinity more in a different universe, one where your mind was kinder to you. One where you didn't have to go. One where I could've known you better. In that world, I would've stolen my time with you without regrets.

Still, I will love you despite the pain. I will always love you despite. Sometimes a little ache is what it takes to love the most beautiful things. I carry this ache with me. Love has never been about avoiding the pain; you bloom bright in spite of it. The falling of the sun promises the presence of the moon. Even the tides follow you in eternal devotion.

You are and always will be worth swallowing the grief.

We may not be so easily understood, but you will forever remain deep in my bones. I carry the memory of you in my breast pocket, closest to my heart. Lingering glances pointed on us often feel sharper than blades, but I will manage them, if only for you. Perhaps no one will ever understand the cosmic link between us.

I feel like I have always known you, and I believe love like that needs no explanation.

III

Part Three

the comedian jokes about transsexuals

I want you to understand but you can't,
    Because you haven't lived it.
    For you, my life is an afterthought, joke, a passing laugh —
    When for me it is
    A news story about a woman shot dead who bled out in her car
    But I know that doesn't matter to you because

For you my life is an afterthought, a joke, a passing laugh
    When for me it is passing comments on
    How it would be better if I was dead than trans
    But I know that doesn't matter to you because to you
    We are no more than a cheap laugh,
    Every day my kin are dying and every day I'm still hearing

Passing comments on
    How it would be better if I was dead than trans
    And you can turn our lives into a joke that never mentions the
    News story about a woman shot dead who bled out in her car
    I want you to understand but you can't
    Because you haven't lived it.

hope, like a trick of the light

The worst emotions are the ones I can't yet put into words. A connection not yet bridged between my mind and the page, breeding deep internal strife.

An emptiness swirls inside me, a pit vast and boundless.

I hold in tears over noodles. I pretend that it will not be so hard to find my way again, but I am set adrift. The ache spreads within me in frigid ice crystals, and I am at risk of surrendering again, to letting myself slip. I am losing the thread. It is harder and harder.

Do I have enough time?

I can't yet let myself believe in hope. I want to be hopeful, I truly do. I want to see the illuminating brightness spreading through the vast tunnel, but I fear it's no more than a passing car, a minute distraction. Only a brief break in the blackness. A trick of the light. The tunnel persists; the end has not come.

A splinter of false hope cuts deeper than any dagger. It pierces and shreds my skin like all fragile things, and I am terrified again, terrified of eternal future in too-loose skin, bones all sharp, heart worn down to stub. I cannot hope, when the image remains, the image of a future where I am still broken, still missing so many pieces.

I am trying to have faith, but I have oft been betrayed by faith before. I do not yet know how to hold hope and not allow it to be a dual-sided blade.

I am tired, and I am so tired of being tired. I am weary-worn, asphalt cracking under eternal tire tracks. I do not know how much longer I can continue before the earth splits and swallows, before the floodgates open and leave nothing behind. I am fit to burst.

I do not want to be defined by my melancholy alone. Still, I am dragged down by stones. I am a river-corpse, not yet fully sunk. I only float.

I have faith in those around me, and I have faith in myself to survive, but surviving life is a life only half-lived. Managing is barely enough.

Lest my heart abandons me, I hope my body will survive. I cannot yet cling to hope. I am so tired of bleeding, so tired of bursting at the seams. Hope is not stable enough a foundation for a heart already made into a wound.

an ode to the university health clinic patient website (elegy for my species)

Today I learn there is holiness in simple things.

I close my eyes and take a gasping breath. I swear I can almost hear angelic choirs singing, a new sort of feeling thrumming in my ears and resonating deep into my bones. I am breathed anew by a god I never thought could live inside me.

It is near impossible to give words to this thing alight in my nerves. I feel every sensation with vibrant electricity, resounding within me. It is light yet dense, a bubble threatening to burst. Rising inside me, from the arch of my foot to the flat of my tongue. It feels as if something is mounting.

The voice of God thrums within me. I am occupied. My veins have learned to be as live as wires. I would spark to the touch, my soul light for the first time I can remember. I ache, but I am no longer splitting at the seams. It feels like healing, like hope.

I trace the inside of my palm with my fingernails, in touch with myself and impossibly alive for the first time. This, this, this. I clench and unclench my fists. I am not my own. Perhaps I never was, expanding beyond the breadth of my own body. The world cannot begin to limit me in my expanse.

No words are enough. Nothing is enough to explain it, for it is simply divinity. Like a promise of life for the first time, a sight of a sprout growing in the desert, life still given upon barren land. I was convinced I was the last of my species, sent to die in these weathered bones, this corpse body, this physical wasteland.

I hold my breath in fear it will all disappear. Hope of survival held, somehow, in a single cursor click. I see the future unfold on angel's wings. A future lived, rather than just a future survived.

This is not the sort of divinity that occupies church walls. This is the divinity known only to the enlightened few. This is the sort of divinity known to needles and glass bottles, clinic walls and self-creation, known only between members of our species. We are self-fabricators. We are citizens of profound and fabulous divinity. The first people to be truly our own. Not broken; yet mended.

I am terrified. I am elated. I am electric, a livewire. I could come apart, liquefy, bones reduced to jelly under holy hands. I am hardly keeping myself together.

The first day, this life inside me echoed small and terrified. Cold concrete under my thighs, brisk air broken by light, winter expansive but not inescapable. It was an act of half-rebellion and wholly an act of becoming. I was desperate and hungry and hurting. I dialed the phone number and felt my breaths like thunder inside my chest. I would crawl my way from this deep cave. My life would no longer be a punishment.

When it was all over, I breathed easy, easy for the first time in a while. Burden broken, maybe, a glimmer of hope. I could feel a lifelong knot unloosening inside me. Despite the bubble of hope, it was no more momentary peace before the onslaught of fear. The realization dawned, a frigid tidal wave rising in my chest: I still would have to go back inside.

I still would have to face them, face everything. The world never knew me as I was. I would have to swallow the pain for the indefinite future. The seas did not part. No holy choir bloomed. The world would not move for me, and I was not strong enough yet to move it. The terror mounted, climbing, my heart screaming to burst through my throat and splatter on pale brick and dusty concrete. Crimson on fresh fallen snow. I could die there, bleeding out in the lawn, hopeful and terrified. Enlightened broken holy vessel. Anyone could take it away. I was so fragile, barely a sprout struggling to survive, struggling to break through the punishing ground into a thicket of weeds. Anything in me could snap, rupturing and sending me spilling out, untethered and vast.

Construction of self, crumbling, on the front-porch step of my parents' house.

This time it is different. I am beginning to construct again, bearing new strength, embarking on a new attempt at a conception of self. One where I fill in the gaps. I am given power and agency and the right to breathe life into a husk of a body I have worked so hard to keep alive. Perhaps, perhaps, my heart will not die inside these flesh-bound walls. Perhaps I could feel alive. Perhaps I could be whole.

Perhaps I already am.

The promise of life with a body I can occupy. The promise of life with a body that I am not afraid to look at in the mirror. A body that is my own, self-created, own hands forming new Adam's clay, occupied wholly with me. Conceived divinity born unto human flesh. No longer emptiness, no longer fear. Bodily autonomy given fresh definition, etching rings of life in my skin. I am embarking on enlightened sight. Divine flesh.

It is hard enough to conceptualize twenty-one years of time half-lived. Experiences missed, not quite captured, a photograph taken from an angle that doesn't give it justice. Sunsets are never captured right, after all. As if I'd placed my finger partially over the lens, obscuring half the picture. The world never knew how to depict me with any justice. I've only ever been making do with half of the image.

I need this. I need this more than I've ever needed anything else, and if I cannot pour my heart out and convince those I love to support me, then I'll figure it out myself.

I tell myself that it is not a sin to believe in hope. I promise myself that is not a punishment to believe in a future, my future. Something I can own and breathe and be. Even this moment, eternal moment, moment most permanent, is not forever. God may have created me, but I create myself. I am incubating. I am waiting for rebirth.

My body is not a grave. My body is not a cage I am forced to live in. My body is a holy reliquary. My body is haven and whole. My body is not a grave. I will not be relegated to a coffin of my half-self.

My body is not a grave.

My body is a garden, and in it my heart will someday bloom.

notes on survival

It's nothing simpler than this.

You will wake up tomorrow, and you will survive.

You will survive, despite.

You will survive, as you have always survived.

That's all that there has ever been, that's all that there is, and that's all there will ever be.

The truth is, there is no way to get through it aside from simply getting through it. You will have to wake up and you will have to live it. You will have to survive it, but you have always survived it, and this is the one and only fact that you need know. Even if that's all that's the only thing left to know anymore.

If you do not yet know it, then etch it into your skin, carve it into your bone, sear it into your brain matter. Memorize it. Know it, hold onto it, dig your nails into it, and even if you bleed from the sharp edges of belief —
    then bleed.

No matter what, don't let that belief go. You will survive, as you have always survived. And you will continue surviving.

You will turn survival into an act as simple as breathing. Survival is an effort, but it is an effort of integration, of looking forward and pushing yourself through. Learning to make surviving fundamental. Survival must become a day-to-day act. It will not get any easier, but you will learn to bear it.

We simplify survival to beginning and end. A three-step process, but we really tell it in two parts. Onset of suffering, end of suffering. Everything in between is left to you. Everything in between, all the ugly parts, all the things that leave you feeling undone and cut loose, open wounds draining, spilling – no one tells you about that.

It's like being left in the wilderness with the promise that one day, someone will come. Rescue will come. The suffering will end. That's the promise: that there's a light at the end of this tunnel, eventually. *We can't tell you what it looks like, but it exists.* And hopefully you won't be dead by the time you reach it.

But until then, you're left in the wilderness, left to your own devices with the hope of a future you cannot begin to conceptualize. Abandoned in the desert with no food or water, given nothing but a roll of yet-developed photographs. You do not even know the images on them, yet - what the future looks like remains blurry. You are left to the in-between and the unknown, and you are expected to survive on the hope that the photographs depict something beautiful — something worth surviving for.

***

Everyone tries to sell secrets on how to survive suffering. Placebo pills, offering nothing aside from the bitter reminder that the suffering persists. The searing reminder that there is no secret to survival. It will not budge. It continues and continues. It keeps going until it doesn't anymore.

Until then, the truth is that no matter what you do, you will have to bear it. This is the only secret worth telling.

I want to say that I have something better to tell you, that there is something unwritten I could write into existence, something to reveal to you, to make it just an inch easier. I wish I could bear the burden, simplify the weight you will have to carry, but that's the hardest thing. It is only time that can heal. You must persist on faith in the future yet seen.

The hardest is realizing that the only difference between night and day is the outlook. There is no secret, no promise, the rising sun could give you.

By the end of the day, I know it feels like you're dragging, carrying the impossible weight of the body bag of your old self, begging for rest, for a moment to breathe. I know you're wishing it all would stop, desiring the simplicity in a pause, craving the soothing absence of burden.

And night sets in, and you're wondering how you'll manage to get up and do it all again. Night sets in, and it all feels ever the more impossible. Wolves of the past come howling. The future seems impossibly thick, swimming through molasses in the hopes of making it to the end – an end you cannot begin to imagine. You're just persisting on no more than the idea of hope. Blank photographs. Rolls of undeveloped film.

* * *

My father used to promise me that no matter what, the sun will rise again tomorrow. No matter what, tomorrow will come, and the sun will crest upon the hills. The day will always come, despite the feeling of night eternal.

In all honesty, I never quite understood that. Despite all best intentions, it always left me with lingering dread. It never felt comforting to me. It felt like a promise, because I knew, and I still know, that even despite the sun rising, I will still have to bear it. The dead are not any lighter with the rising of the sun.

I will drag the corpse of myself with me. The night will not rid me of the past nor simplify the present. The morning will not present a new world or easier challenges. You will not be reborn when you wake.

I am sure, in times like this, the weight of your own flesh feels like stones stitched to your ankles, dragging you ever downwards.

I am sorry to tell you, more than anything else, that the sun will rise again tomorrow. Tomorrow, the sun will rise again, and you will have to bear it. The past will still hang like a ghost in the doorway. The corpses will remain unburied.

The only difference between night and day is the outlook.

Tomorrow, when the sun rises, it's likely that it will feel the same. Maybe, if you're lucky – and I hope you are – the weight will feel a little lighter, the air less choking, the walls a little wider. But in all likelihood, it will feel the same. Despite the night's rest, you will feel exhausted. Even through the night, you have been dragging your past selves, long since dead. Even your sleeping body fights to keep you alive.

The rise of the sun will not make any of that any easier.

But I see it like this: you have two choices. You can survive it, or you can let yourself collapse under the weight.

You can bear it, or you can break.

I know it often feels easier to break. There's an undeniable allure to giving up. Surrender, so you won't have to keep fighting. The day ahead feels like a promise of weight. Even in the sunlight, you are tasked with the impossible task of survival. You will want to relent. You will face familiar and new obstacles, steep and shallow, daunting and unrelenting. The hits will keep coming. There is no use in fighting the tide.

Truth is, the only promise that the day can give you is the promise of the passage of time. Night has passed, day is born, the past has breached forward into the present. The sun rises, despite.

Time has continued, as it will always continue. Despite it all, we cannot make it stop. We cannot slow the ticking clock behind all of us.

I have come to find comfort in that. You can rely on time like you can rely on water. Time, beyond everything, will always continue. Even when you cannot continue, time will. Time and her vast, unceasing stream. Put your trust in her. She will carry you through.

* * *

I am learning to surrender to the stream of time. In the morning, when the sun rises and the day promises weight impossible, almost too heavy to carry, then I live for my future self. I cannot change the now, so I live for the later.

These days, I'm starting to believe I'm one of the world's first time-travelers. I'm living in the future. I'm an architect planning a future life, planning on the land where the building of my inevitable self will one day stand.

I spend a great deal of time in the future, blocking out the halls and walls of memory for a life I will soon live. Like painting a nursery, I am creating a space for a self not yet born. *Here is the space I will occupy, here is the place I will live.* I am moving and planning, filling in the blanks. I am deliberate in what I am giving to my future self. Most of the time, what I give him is no more than surviving. This is enough.

Close and so impossibly far away, I surrender to time, let her carry me downwards, forward into self. Further into future.

***

I conceptualize the coming house of my heart before it has even been built. I sketch my future into being with patient dedication. I overlook no detail in constructing this house, slowly filling in all the gaps.

These are the walls I will trace with older hands. This is the sofa I will one day sit in. My body will sink into this leather in a way I cannot begin to understand, but I can understand the sofa. I cannot picture myself, so I picture the objects, the material world of promised occupance. I will imagine the spaces in-between, the ones I will one day fill.

These efforts are a promise. A promise that if I create a space, if I manage to survive, I will one day get to live there. If the future is waiting, then my only task is to survive the now.

I cannot begin to imagine my body occupying the world, so I will imagine the sofa. I will imagine the cutlery. I will imagine the mattress, the way my body will one day press into it. I conceptualize the in-betweens. When I cannot have faith in my body, I will put my faith in material promises of future.

I am creating a life I will some day be able to exist within. I will give myself the promise that life can one day bear me as I have learned to bear it.

***

I am surviving, if anything, for my future self. Even if I cannot yet see him, even if I cannot yet imagine his face, or understand his heart, or conceptualize the way he moves through the world, I continue my diligent work. I am creating a space for him to live. Today, and all days, I bear it for him.

I bear it for him, and I let time carry me forward. Time, send me home, to a world I hope will one day be mine.

Send me home, towards myself, where I know I am waiting.

IV

Part Four

the growing-up itch

This is hard to admit, to any person, and even harder to admit to myself. Yet, I still write it down, equal quiet and loud as I etch it into existence with fingers praying on plastic keys. Spacebar communion. Confessional on dark screen, like peeling my skin and stretching my ribs to bare myself to the God known only to laptops and leatherbound journals. Writing, prayer, confessional. Equal in desperation and faith.

This is what I tell myself.

An act of writing can feel so easy as breathing and yet so painful as bleeding, spilling from me in free-fall, the catharsis of an exhale that leaves me aching, stripped bare and exposed within the vaulted walls of a church or a page – there is no difference.

I know the written word like many know God. So, consider this an act of prayer.

Imagine this spoken best in the halls of a church or in the breathing walls of a confessional booth. Imagine this, too, with the struggled whisper of a secret and the desperation of a midnight phone call to an old friend.

In life, I have often been a lonely person. Perhaps the feeling isn't simply loneliness — it's loneliness coupled with lack of understanding, the feeling that no one has ever wanted to know the person hiding beneath my skin. A great deal of the time, I didn't even want to know the person held within me, leaving me trapped inside myself, caged in bone prison, bound with sinew. I fled from self, sheltering from the sharp edges of self-perception, desperate to avoid understanding.

Even now, I am not yet sure if I know myself. Perhaps I am beginning to. I believe I may only ever know myself in momentary breaths, self-actualization that comes more like a punch than a stark awakening. It has no permanence. It's a cold flush and it fades before my next heartbeat. There it goes, see? I've lost myself again.

* * *

I don't ache over childhood because I believe that most children spend childhood lonely, occupied by the expanse of a person growing inside little bones, stretching to burst forth and be free; be known and be seen. Children cannot begin to know each other, despite best attempts. We are all too complex and self-occupied, barely growing roots yet constantly expanding. We are root systems of plants that have barely reached the surface — you will not know unless you dig.

Even as adults, to know is really an act of desperation, and to be known is a wish.

Nonetheless, I was a lonely child. As a child, I felt like an overfull glass, water droplets spilling over the rim. I spent long days whispering into oak and mud, asking to be known by the earth if nothing else. Flesh could not know me, so I relied on the steady constant of terra firma.

(I learned, eventually, the earth is a better listener than a talker.)

I occupied my mind rather than my body, my head rather than my heart. My emotions have oft felt like roots stretching past me into the ground, nerve endings I cannot access. Feelings unbeknownst to me, until when I least expect them. The feelings come jumbled, in brief and terrifying abstracts, intense and furious.

As a child, I held on to what I could. I sought to find something stable to hold onto, an anchor point for my wavering heart. Just as I do now, I relied intensely on the power of words, my one and only foothold, solid ground in earthquake territory. I remained lost in the mazes of my mind and I wrote stories, stories of people lost and found, hurt and healing, loved and longed for. Stories of people wanted and people fully understood.

Above all, I craved belonging, so I wrote of belonging. I etched into the world what I did not yet see or feel.

(It is not a habit I have abandoned as an adult.)

* * *

I am cresting onto a wave of adulthood, still finding my footing, so I feel not yet equipped to speak of my young adulthood in a way that offers much grace or patience. Still, I will tell you what I know. I am not sure how much good it will do.

Every teenager bursts forth with emotions like a dam threatening to crack, but my vibrant, heaving, frantic emotions were little help when aided by the crises of young adulthood.

Like everyone else, I did the best I could. I fit into seams between walls and gaps between floorboards, echoing and seeking recognition. See me, know me, want me, hold me. Feeling known, even if known in pieces — known broken, known bruised — felt as good as the hands of the divine. I craved adoration, and if I couldn't have it, then I would leave claw marks on the walls as proof that I was there at all.

Even if to be known was to be carved open and cast aside, I took it, hungry for proof I existed anywhere aside from within my own body. My sweetest divine sacrament, consume my flesh and know me as I am.

I mistook the feeling of being known for the feeling of being loved. I let myself be taken apart, pieces of me stolen and warped by hungry hands. Consumption and hunger felt like desire, and I took anything I could get. To be something to someone, to anyone, was enough. I would take a stray glance with the same desperation that I'd take a punch to the jaw or a kiss on the cheek.

To be anything was enough. To be anyone was enough.

Above all, I wrote. I wrote voraciously, my mind a dam ever-bursting forth with words, threatening to crack under the pressure. My body could barely occupy it. I was convinced nothing I wrote meant anything, more a form of begging to be allowed the grace to exist, as if the words on the page could give me the release the world held back. Even when I wasn't writing things down, I wrote in the hollow halls of my mind, words echoing to vast and unoccupied space. It had nowhere to go, drifting inside me, so I carried it.

The page was a place to spill. Writing was prayer, punishment, penance for lives I tried to live and left behind. I was always asking for forgiveness for ancient sins. I was always trying to be someone else. It was the only way I felt I could exist in entirety, painting myself, in all my emptiness and fears, through words.

***

I think the truth is I have always been terrified nothing I do will ever matter.

I remember the first time I heard those words. *Seven billion.* My fourth-grade teacher held up a magazine with the words plastered across the cover, somehow both hopeful and damning. As a child, you cannot even begin to comprehend that number. How could you? A hundred people in your grade feels like the entirety of the world.

How could seven billion people really exist? I kept asking myself, where could they even live? Where did they all fit? There surely couldn't be enough space for that many people.

It felt like drowning. A sea of people, surrounded me, all sides and all corners, like people could come raining from the sky.

Could I ever really exist? Had I ever really existed, at all?

How does a droplet of water in the ocean even begin to define itself, to be known, to be something? It is only one in an endless mass, a vast and expansive sea. I felt shapeless, formless. I was lost, and I would never be found.

In seven billion, where could I begin to matter?

I was a worried child. I am a worried adult. I ponder meaning, purpose, action. I take on tasks too big for my mind to comprehend, trying to swallow an understanding of a world daunting and boundless, hoping against hope to find a foothold, an inkling of solace. A singular fragment of clarity or meaning.

I want to create. I want to be something, do something, mean something. But if I am only a droplet, then where would I ever begin?

* * *

I make this promise, to put words to page. I make the promise that the act can be enough. Even if the words mean nothing, even if it is simply spilling, a mark of desperation by an eternally worried man. It can mean nothing and still be something. By putting words down, I am at least creating a mark of existence.

A mark that these thoughts ever were, that I ever was.

I define myself, carve myself into the background of the world with hungry desperation to prove the meaning of my existence. To mark that there was a purpose behind putting the atoms that comprise me together before I am taken apart and returned to the universe again, no more than recycled dust to the cosmos.

To exist simply for the sake of existence is not enough. I have to prove that I was here, that I was something. That in a sea of seven billion, that I was a molecule all my own.

Even if the words mean nothing, even if I am leaving my claw marks on useless walls, even if they are only desperate scratches, at least I have proven that these thoughts — these words — lived and breathed in me.

And in that way, they meant something, and so did I.

* * *

They call this feeling introspection, I think. It's never been the right word. Thoughtful thought. Rumination. Trapped in my own mind, boiling over with the weight of emotion and cognition, impossible to speak but too heavy to hold.

It should be a blessing. Most days, I drown under it.

For my whole life, it's as if I've been trapped inside my mind. Even if I try to speak it out loud, to tell everyone, I remain always brimming full and sinking under the weight of my own thoughts.

I witness the world around me, moving and existing, breathing like an organ itself, humans in unison. A singular heart beating. It feels a punishment, to be burdened with self-awareness, so sharp it cuts me through.

In these recent months of endless preoccupation with the state of everything, I have struggled to come up with names for this time in my life. A period defined by terrible loneliness yet immeasurable pride. The in-between. The grey area. Meaningful nothing. Beautiful, bright, sharp, terrifying existence. Painful, teeming with joy, motivated yet entirely exhausted. Entirely incomplete yet always searching.

It is not so simply wrapped up in the idea of young adulthood. Many of those around me are experiencing the same years in vastly different shades than I am, leaving me feeling as if I am living an entirely different life than everyone else. They experience; I am forced to notice everything, and relegated to observation.

These days, I've given the feeling another name, born from patient and careful study. *The growing-up itch.* It's not an itch you can scratch, not a hunger you can sate. It looms and lingers, not punishing, fabulously gentle — yet far from polite. It is an endless and imminent reminder of the work that is left to be done, the life that has yet to be lived. I am patient, but there is something humming electric beneath my skin, a version of me lying in wait that I am building a future for. An itch.

It's a state of in-betweens, an impossibility in itself, and one I cannot begin to illuminate in easy terms. Every word offered is a desperate stab into vast blackness.

I am an engineer of future self. I am both architect and gardener, churning raw earth into clay and encouraging blooms to sprout. The land on which my life will flourish will not come naturally, and it will not come with ease. I must plant seeds and construct the halls in which I will soon move through.

In my state of in-betweens, I practice introspection religiously. I am learning to know myself as some know faith. I have taken to the practice of self-worship in simple tasks. Breathing functions as prayer, each step a devotional hymn, each day lived a day sainted in the past for the structure I am continually building.

I crave to no longer be in-between. I am a bloom that seeks desperately to breach the earth and see the sun again — maybe even, for the first time.

I used to ache to be something. These days, I ache only to be.

I feel kinship with weeds, who pursue life before beauty, expansion before aesthetic. For weeds, beauty is a coincidence. If I am beautiful, it will be the product of my existence, a result rather than a foundation. A blessing, rather than a necessity.

The growing up itch is a state of in-betweens, a state of impatience and of insatiable hunger. The growing up itch looks forward into future and witnesses joy, but it does not yet know how to arrive there.

I am happy now, but the architect can only be so happy with an incomplete cathedral. My cells buzz and push for a path forward.

My breath speaks in in-betweens and my body lacks understanding. I am myself only as I know myself today, but I realize that this version of me is not yet whole. I am undermined by the simple fact of stasis.

It is not enough.

The growing-up itch is melancholic. Grey areas so often are, lacking answers, leaving a bittersweet taste beneath my tongue. I am not often sad, not anymore. Not like I used to be, pierced through and screaming. I feel as defined as a drawing half-shaded, a painting half complete. Beautiful but not finished; I have pride in how far I have come, pride in my survival and constant persistence, but I am not yet done. Unfinished state of self held in seeming permanent stasis.

I know my parts, my pieces. I am filling in the gaps, but as I begin to fill the gaps, empty space seems to spawn more empty space. More and more, I find parts unfulfilled. Still, I am not empty — I am as whole as the moment allows. A house under construction is still a house, no matter how complete. I tell myself this again and again, a mantra or prayer, a promise or a wish.

I am whole with myself, filled up and brimming. I am hungry and starving and well-fed. I watch sunsets from the overlook of the main road through my little town and I wonder, I think, I think and I wonder. I contemplate the future. The growing up itch vibrates inside me but I force myself to be still. I feel fit to burst. I find myself crying. I am always crying.

In these days, I begin to see the pieces I am missing, but I have no intention of filling in the gaps with the artificial. I tried for so long to make myself whole with false gods, to occupy my heart with love that left structural damage. These days, there is no echoing, no pretending. I crave only the literal and the real.

The house I am building will come in time.

* * *

To tell you the truth, to ache would be simpler. To hurt would allow suffering. Hurt would warrant fits and screaming and the holy catharsis of tears. I don't find suffering in these days occupied by long in-betweens. It is simply stasis. It just is.

I am overwhelmed by sheer breadth of emotion but there are few words to describe them. Just as my childhood self, my emotions have never come labeled in neat, ordered little boxes. I can begin to comprehend myself but I always end up losing the thread all over again. I don't feel in ways so simple, leaning instead towards confusing concoctions of emotions that can be solved only in putting words to page in a frenzied attempt for self-actualization. Even still, I'm grasping at straws.

I have begun to accept that I can know everything and yet know nothing at all. To sate the itch, this is what I believe. While I can begin to splice and pick it apart, examine the roots that create the feeling, by breaking it apart I lose the meaning. I end up right back where I started. The meaning is as circular and abstract as it ever was. I am left with all beginnings and no endings, and a brain worked into overdrive in attempting to understand.

I was an emotional child. I am an emotional adult. Sometimes, I tell myself, this is a product of feeling emotions differently, or more, than other people. Yet, I'm sure I'm not the only one who feels this way. My whole life, I have been sure I am not the only person who feels like this. I hope this is not only sheer optimism — seven billion, after all. The world is too big for no one else to understand.

But really, what am I to do with that? Am I simply to live with an understanding that I am alone now, and I might be alone for time indefinite? And despite that, am I to continue to have an ever-present, frustratingly optimistic hope that there is someone out there who feels the same?

So I write.

That's really all it ever comes down to. That's always where it returns, always where the road leads. Any question, any hurt, there is only one ending to it all. I find all answers, all solutions, all secrets, in writing.

It is a Bible I can write myself. Holy texts that come from my own hands and my own heart. I suppose in that way, God is both in myself and in the page.

I am guided ever-constant by my North Star. Yet, my North Star expects me to find the answers, to give them to myself. I cannot find the answers out there in the world. I cannot solve these problems with the help of others. No one and nothing can give me the satisfaction I seek more than the satisfaction I receive from putting thought to page, in all its' impossibly impenetrable glory. Because that's all it is, abstraction traced and transformed.

I take it all - the impossibilities, the frustrations, the madness, the loneliness, and I turn it into something, something that I hope matters. Writing is a prayer that I can take the futilities of life and turn them into something legible, but more than that — something meaningful.

I draft and compose confessionals in the hope that anyone speaks the language. For most of my life, I have hardly been able to fathom the idea of exposing the written word to the world. Not in pure, raw form. It is best spoken to the earth alone. The earth listens, and it offers no judgment. The world might not understand.

It is hard enough, to facilitate the birth between mind and page. To release it to the world, to let them see and hear me, all of me. The idea is terrifyingly daunting. I — like every other person who has ever created anything in the history of time — fear the sour rejection of misunderstanding.

But still, I write. I write and I hope for understanding on the horizon.

And for the meantime, I build.

I build, and I release myself in writing, and I wonder if it might ever be read by anyone who feels the same. I wonder if anyone else feels the growing up itch, the way it thrums under your skin like a second heart or an electric wire.

Writing is not so easy a religion to share. Writing is an autopsy on national broadcast television.

I carve my heart out and I hope someone else might look back and see something familiar in the bloodstains.

two mangoes

in his hands, he holds
    two mangoes.
      he asks you if they are enough.
      he is still good,
      despite what you know
      that you have put him through.

born artist

Born artist.
    I came into this world with my spine carved with words.
    Bone-deep tattooed ink,
    prophesy of past, present, future.
    Born artist.
    Divine guidance; personal scripture.
    I am still unfolding to myself,
    I am always under construction,
    New vision of self going up catty-corner to the old,
    All of us, etched with same fundamental truth,
    Born artist.
    Each vein marked with divine scripture,
    Born artist,
    So I am stitching my own thread
    into the delicate fibers of creation.

born witness

Revelation.

An ordinary window can be stained glass if the light hits it just right.

I walk this route every day, but I've never seen this before. Green bottle glass reflects against the ice-kissed tar of the crosswalk, glittering in the melting snow like emeralds. Refracted light, I think, the kind that makes rainbows. More luminous than the window itself. Window panes transform the asphalt into the mortar of stained-glass churches; holy.

Asphalt consecrated into holy ground.

Lately I have become a careful student of the world in motion around me. It is impossibly, punishingly fast. I am trying to slow it down. I move through the world deliberately, aware of even the shifting of particles around me; displacement of air, the way my body occupies a space.

Something is unfolding before me; a night-bloom, shy to daylight. For the first time, I am still enough to notice it. I am transfixed by each minute second. There is a tenderness to every detail. It goes so easily overlooked.

In each minute second, I am discovering residual divinity, etched in everything. Grand constructions. Holy particulate.

I am reminded of Impressionist paintings. From afar, the composition smears and blurs into a whole image, one resolutely sure of itself, delicate detail more whisper than spoken word. But the closer you go, the brushstrokes become illumined, the motion of the creator revealed, like the opening of a bloom. The fundamental strings of the artist's design. These are the parts of the painting I spend the most time with. That's where the soul of the artist remains, even when long since gone.

A brushstroke is a fingerprint. There is a patience to Van Gogh and a tenderness to Cassatt. There is a heart, a deliberateness, behind the gesture of a quick dab of oil or a sweeping thicket of gouache. Intentionality. Purpose. Quick or conscious, energetic or impossibly patient. This is where the heart resides. You discover more about the meaning in a simple stroke of paint than in the image entire.

Behind the picture plane, the grand intention is revealed in the minute and finite details. The emerald asphalt tells me more about God than any divine treatise. No holy book has ever captured this.

If there is a grand narrator, an omnipotent spirit beyond this world, then this is the greatest evidence of it. An ordinary window and ordinary asphalt. Assign it by any name, and it is still the same. If it exists, this is where the holy hides, in the overlooked. In the ordinary window that turns the asphalt into emeralds.

I find myself drawn most to the concept of the angelic. I am enamored by their tenderness, equal only to their wrath. My belief is less scriptural and more self-assured, but I am beginning to see angels in all things. Invisible, minute players on a grand stage.

There are angels hiding everywhere. I am captured gentle by the angel of the crosswalk, angel of the emerald light.

Perhaps this is what religion has always been about. The very fabric of faith. The little things. I had anticipated conceptual *Revelation* to come explosive, more firework than whisper. Nonetheless, I am born witness to quiet revelation. Only a murmur. Angelic intervention as delicate as dove wings, quiet as hummingbird heart.

I sought that capital-R Revelation more days than I can count. I remember girls bursting into tears, kneeling on linoleum and wracked by sobs, overcome by some divine presence I had no awareness of. They were enveloped by a holy touch that never reached out to me. Perhaps I was always looking too high. The heavens too lofty a goal for my earthly form. Searching in the cosmos has always felt like surrendering to being swallowed.

It's no church-camp awakening or holy-handed miracle, but still, I do I feel a bodily presence of the sacred. Maybe not God proper – the capital G kind, but I do find remnants of the holy here. Shattered fragments.

The awakening imparted to me is little more a quiet tug to the shirtsleeve. Nothing more than an urge. To slow down; to bear witness to the reflections. *Take a breath and look.*

* * *

I believe most in the angels of small things. Angels of crosswalks, angels of sneakers, angels of telephone poles. Angels of chimneys and lightbulbs and lip balm. Small-time angels, connecting the in-betweens with invisible strings. Perhaps there are angels for the larger things, but these are the ones I like best, the angels often missed.

The set designers behind the production, constructing the grand image we are too close to understand. We act only as characters upon the divine's grand, theatrical stage. *We are merely players.*

(I suppose we do always return to those age-old revelations. Nothing truly new, just born again.)

Evidence of divine creation or intervention always acts on a much smaller scale. I think I forgot to look for the brushstrokes. That's where the angels hide.

I have always preferred the sort of godliness you can bundle up and tuck in your pocket. I always liked things best when you can carry them with you.

I am memorizing the divine's great mundanity. I am tracing common paths with careful steps. There are angels hiding here.

Always angels, everywhere. Crosswalk angel, teach me how to peer into the glass and find myself again. Show me what it all means.

I offer my surrender. Cast me in emerald; bear me witness to something beyond me.

I want to carry that reflection of sun inside me.

melody of meaningless nothing

In my quiet moments, I am discovering countless truths.

My mind is packed full with tangled-yarn thoughts. The artist is easily consumed within themselves. Each breath weaved with the red-hot fiber of creation. I am always at risk of losing myself. My mind, this expansive, vast lake. The endless depth of the glass-water reflecting pool; I am always testing the limits.

I've an awful habit of self-reflection - meaningless musing, the artist's best-loved habit, pacing the same old floorboards in hope of finding a new pattern. Evaluating and re-evaluating until I've tangled myself past recognition. Only going in circles. Tracing new shapes on the wall, lost to myself.

More and more these days, I am letting myself succumb. I follow the endless string and hope to catch a few thoughts worth penning into existence. Something that means something, I hope. Maybe no one understands, but I hope they do. It becomes a prayer.

The fiber of creation inside me is always easy to ignore. A murmur resonating inside the cathedral of my bones. So quiet, it has always been easy to bury within. The human heart is often distracted, the mind easily occupied. It is so easy to drown out a whisper, and the universe is so loud. The world never ceases; impossible blur, rising tide. I am - painfully - teaching myself to how to slow down. I force silence. I count breaths. I embrace the meaningless moments, their quiet melodies. Little whispers from the great beyond, revealing their secrets to me.

I am transfixed in these moments, in the in-betweens: the drive home from the coffee shop, the walk home from class, the last breaths taken before sleep. I notice more and more every day.

We are animal beings occupied by entire universes of nothing. I wonder the last time I paid attention with total reverence to the world around me. We offer our lives no patience, no reflection. We run from the in-betweens or pack them so full that they disappear. We pack ourselves into little suitcases and tuck them underneath our bed frames.

I hope one day to unpack the entirety of myself.

* * *

This is the most fragile I have been. My openness leaves me a fresh wound. I bloom energy as red as blood. Most days, I am convinced others can see right through me. I am impossibly vulnerable, jam-packed and eternally transparent.

I am seeking home. I am building cathedrals of bluebird bones, grandiosity on weak foundations. I am inhabiting gaps and smoothing over pains like untidy sheets, trying my best to live in my dissatisfactions. Perhaps the halls of reflection are the only chambers safe enough to inhabit. Inside my mind, I am sheltered .

I am seeking silence. I am unlearning the practice of swallowing days like cough medicine. I am embracing my simple life, my in-betweens. Bite-sized pains and emotions carefully wrapped. Perhaps I have always been a small soul, bearing a heart that functions best in nooks and crannies.

Silence brings forth new light. Watershed of words. The floodgates release and breathe creation into existence.

We have entered the coldest months of winter. I always remember January for her continuance, her biting cold, her persistent permanence. She cuts deep. In the past, I have found January the hardest to survive, the bitterest pill to swallow of all of the months. I have understood January as an unclimbable mountain, looking down the barrel at the year ahead. I have never known where to begin in a month that feels made all up of endings. January is harsh and brutal, rarely gentle, fit for loneliness and bitter cold filling the empty gaps in between.

January leaves you aching, always wanting. Fractured, frigid winter wind blowing through disconnected pieces. She has always revealed my weaknesses, always left me heartbroken.

This January, I am suffering from a constant and continual sense of understanding. I come to and the world swarms around me, splintered and shattered and pointing down. Jagged, hungry teeth. The two-sided blade of perception digs into the shallow muscle that shields the fragile bone underneath. Every breath spears me through

Despite the great precipice of perception, I am not finding answers. I am finding only more questions, more conundrums, and countless truths.

Perhaps I have too much time on my hands. I live a life well-contemplated, a life cut and spliced into little pieces. Moments fit for microscopic study. I seek meaning. The world remains a mirage. My mind evades my own understanding. I keep ending up in the same place again — perhaps I've only ever been walking in circles.

***

In my slow, brutal January, I am trying to notice it all. I am burdened with perception, a storm that never quells. I cannot know everything, so I will tuck these moments into little drawers for safe-keeping. Perhaps they will reveal themselves in time.

I am seeking to memorize all of it, each and every feeling. Numb fingers gripping wool sweater, tracing the metal bars of the ramp at the library. Material sensation, awash in soft light and illumined in color. I set this aside for further observation.

Everyday, I am seeing things for the first time. I am committing these realizations to memory, cataloguing everything and yet nothing at all. I am cataloguing meaninglessness. I am cataloguing mundanity. I am ear-marking the ordinary for further study. Memorization facilitates creation. Words climb from deep within, locust plague. In a world where I am forced to recognize, I endure by remembering.

I am always writing. Every still moment, every second of in-between, I am writing. I am etching on the margins in the pages of my memory. The words come in free-fall, no longer a leaky faucet; great watershed of creation. No efforts to direct the flow or dam it has had any success. I have stopped trying. The beams of sunlight radiate in strings of words, the snow dusts in long and winding sentences. The world blooms around me and the writing comes with it. The cliffs of my mind have splintered, and the words have come, endless — *terrifyingly* endless. I cannot even begin to try to catch up with them. I am outrun by the flood of untethered creation, always at risk of drowning.

Most of the time, my writing does not make it to the page. My mind births writing stillborn, breathing momentary before it dissipates into air. The words speak in gasping breaths, curling around the bounds of my mind before releasing. I desire no longer to catch up. Instead, I dig through the reaches of memory in a desperate attempt to recall, knowing it is already gone.

I wake up buried in thought and I go to sleep adrift in a sea of fragmented consciousness.

I try to catch everything I can, but it is like trying to count raindrops in a downpour, studying shooting stars in a meteor shower. One cannot begin to record every detail of an infinity.

In these moments, I notice how everyone moves so fast, everyone so rarely taking notice of the spaces in-between. I am fixated on the little details, the things permanent and transient. I am noticing the way the slush of the melting snow slides under my boots, neither liquid nor solid, displaced and broken, spread over leather like butter on toast.

I am noticing the freckles of the girl across the table, peeking from the top of her mask. Fallen stars. Dusting of snow. I am starting to believe that everyone is bursting forth with something they let no one else see. I am obsessed with this, this subtle and imperfect beauty. I am noticing the way the snow falls from the shaking trees, dripping like rain. I file that away, staring up into the filtered sun through the branches. I hold my breath. I am slower than the movement of the world around me. Utterly still. Everything rushes past.

If the world is whitewater, then I am a sole, unmoving stone.

I am noticing every person, every little glance. I am noticing the flush of color of someone's clothes on the barren, white landscape. A snow bloom. I am noticing how others move through and occupy the world; the subtle expressions that denote thought, pain, loneliness, love. Everyone existing in a world their own, totally inaccessible to me. I am noticing the carelessness in which others occupy the spaces in which they exist. I am trying to contradict that by the sheer fact of my being.

I seek to reach out through words. Bounds of human existence breached by creation's gentle fingers. I desire connection, if only here.

In all of this, I am noticing something I have yet to give words to. I have never been the best at describing my own emotions, not in such simple terms. My heart experiences emotion best in abstracts, displaced between body and soul, incomplete and ethereal. But this feeling, whatever it is, is the worst of them all, evading capture even in words. Every day, I partake in the endless chase, spilling words onto keyboards and through ink, desperately reaching, grasping for name, for a word to slip through. Something to hold onto.

I have not even begun to grasp it. How can you write something down you can barely begin to describe? I am relegated to documenting. Meaning hides in every breath. These moments will never be the same. Life is always changing. Movement persists. A moment of stillness is enough to change it all. More and more, I am lost within myself.

The words often mean nothing. I am attempting, desperately, to capture a fleeting thought, an ephemeral memory, the face of an old friend in a photograph whose name I can't quite remember; the momentary reflection in the glass left by the setting sun. In a second, the moment will pass, already long gone.

I am trying to learn the impossible act of capturing a fleeting memory. Most of the Impressionists only made preparatory paintings when out in the countryside. *En plein air.* I'm beginning to understand why. Offer it full attention, and you'll miss the moment entirely. You can never capture that glint quite right, and you'll never be able to describe it again. It will only ever exist in that brief and transient second. Only a breath. No more than a single blink.

I am left to surrender to the tide, capturing the torrential flood in tiny jars. For the first time in my life, I feel utterly, shockingly awake. I am trying to trap the tide in glass, trying to collect something to suggest presence or memory. I record my small existence in words. I hope, desperately, that this will be enough.

I am forced to remember that I exist. I was under the impression that I was aware of it before this, but this is entirely new. This is life in technicolor.

I am practicing taking the silence in. I am beginning with small seconds. I still on the sidewalk, face turned upwards to the sun. I count breaths. I am reminded of the sheer fact of my existence. Seconds tick by. I memorize this, the warmth on my cold-nipped face, the roughness of my palms. I close my eyes and trace the heartlines, following them to the faultlines of the earth itself. The world that expands out from me, into the impossible bounds of the universe.

In these moments, words flood the halls of my memory, desperate to escape. I etch out the broad strokes of this memory in my mind, the warmth of the sun against a backdrop of bitter January cold, the way my toes curl forward and heels press backward. Balance. I detect presence in my mind, recording a moment of singular and total consciousness.

It feels like everything and nothing at all. Before I know it, I am crying. I will never remember why.

I am desperate to record the words as they come. Before, it felt easier to let them shrink away into nothing, to release them and leave them to the mercy of the wind, scattered. I don't know how long I've been doing it for, how long I've drifted like this. I never remember beginning, and I can't imagine it will ever end. It's a passive act, as simple as breathing, done with the same automation as how a body pumps blood through the veins. Fragments, liquid thought. Writing, like cataloguing water. I am still trying to describe the glimmer, the way it rubs the pebbles smooth with a lover's gentle dedication.

The beauty comes in the continual feeling of never getting it quite right. Writing is not a reflection or a photograph. It is far more abstract. This is something cosmic. If I am lucky, I will spend the rest of my life trying to figure this out.

To me, writing has never been about forcing my mind to create something. I ask nothing of my mind when I embark upon the page. I do not pull any strings. It is nothing more than letting go. Close your eyes and breathe. Find the center. Release. Separate the soul from the consciousness and let the fingers do everything else.

Flowers bloom without permission of the dirt. The words come before I even know them.

hopeful, happy, ugly

It's a dull ache that comes from teaching yourself to breathe a scream.

These days, I swallow pain like a bubble. I let it decompose inside me. Some pain is fruitful, feeding the worms and fungi, nourishing the earth, but sometimes, pain is plastic. It takes years to decompose, settling inside my hollow heart like a stone.

I promise myself that in time, less pain will settle. Less pain will sink.

One day, I will learn to let it float. To stop breathing screams, to at last release them.

I know I will hurt, and I will hurt profound. I will continue to lose, and I will continue to ache. The weights of the past won't budge in their presence, but my hurt will feed all that grows within me, offering new blooms. It always has. Anguish like this breeds fertile earth for future happiness.

Pain produces painful poems – both poems hard to read, and hard to write. Loneliness, too, produces lonely poems. I do not want to write painful poems or lonely poems anymore. I want to write hopeful poems, poems in waiting, poems that understand transience and allow life to even the grayest areas. I want, need, crave Hopeful. I cannot find hope often, so I will write it into being.

I will deliver my own hope - not in gift-wrapped, pretty-perfect packages. I will scratch and bleed and claw hope into existence. It will be mine and mine own.

I want Hopeful *ugly*. I want Hopeful before the hope comes through. Let hopefulness exist before the word *hope* is even conceived. Let it breathe and bleed and paint the air.

I know, at some point in my life, I will be Happy. True Happy. The honest Happy — the ugly kind. Happy all stitched up and scabbed. Happy with gaps, happy on the mend. Ugly Happy.

Happy that's new to the movies and the novels. The kind of Happiness you can't quite romanticize. It's not picture-perfect. It's the sort of happy that doesn't pretend. The sort of Happy that doesn't leave promises where it can't give.

But it's enough. It's more than enough.

I want the sort of Happiness that knows wholeness is relative. Wholeness is a decision, a promise, a compromise. Wholeness never looks quite how you expected.

Wholeness is born when you decide you are whole enough; that this is enough. It's up to you to decide. You can be whole, even broken. Wholeness is relative. Happiness is relative. This moment is relative. *You are whole, you have always been.*

Future happy, promised happy, ugly happy — I carry it all within myself. All of it, waiting to be born, held inside this weary, faithful body. I feed pain to the worms and hope something happy sprouts from this damp, soaking earth.

I bloom flowers from fertile scars. Truth is, I have always bloomed.

***

Acknowledgments

Dear reader,

When I was younger, I never thought that I would publish work. It was unfathomable to me, the idea of putting my writing out there. It seemed impossibly vulnerable. For a long time, I disregarded the idea entirely. Writing, for me, was to be kept a secret. Shared between myself and a few lucky people — if any. I could never imagine the idea of publishing a book or releasing it to the hands of strangers.

In high school, I put together a collection of poetry, called *a girl is a gun*, just to see my current body of work together. Mostly, I made it to see if I could do it. Only a couple of people past myself read it. It lived and died within my Google Drive, where it still resides. Although my work has long since changed and grown past that, as have I, I firmly believe that the heart of that collection lives and breathes inside *Ugly Happy*. Life is almost always about proving ourselves wrong.

As I am writing this, this book is not yet finished. Yet, every day, it inches closer and closer to completion. For the past weeks and months, it has become an obsession. Even when I'm not working on it, I'm thinking about it. I will apologize to my mother in advance because I have missed a class (or two) in pursuit of working on writing and working on this book. I hope you can forgive me for that, as I have felt immense pressure, deep in my bones, to put this out into the world. It had to be born. It itched inside me with the desperation of something hatching in my bones.

I was under the impression that the acknowledgments section of a book was the sort of thing only allowed to "established" writers — people with editors and the like to thank. It seemed like the sort of thing only published writers could do. But I've come recently to understand that self-publishing is sort of like birth without a midwife. I've still created life, and there is much to acknowledge. I will attempt to scratch the surface of my gratitude, but these words will never be enough to express the depth of it, so take them with that in mind.

First, I'd like to thank my parents, for always tirelessly supporting me and my writing. Thank you, Mom, for always letting me read my poems to you and always showing me so much love. You were one of the first champions of my writing, even before I knew you as my Mom. Thank you, Dad, for always encouraging me to write and to pursue my passion, no matter how hard it might be in the future. Thank you for always pushing me, even when I fought like hell against it. Thank you for never, ever giving up on me.

Thank you to my grandparents, Larry and Kathleen, for reading years of my work (no matter how bad) and always showing me love, kindness, and support. Thank you for valuing my poetry enough to frame it and hang it on your wall. You both are one of the main reasons I am the writer I am today, and you have my eternal gratitude.

Thank you to my forever fairy godmother, Carrie, for always being in my corner, listening to me, and supporting my creative drive. You have nurtured a love for art in me unparalleled by anyone else I've ever known. I am so grateful I know you.

Thank you to every educator who has ever supported me and offered me faith and guidance, but especially: thank you, Carol Hendry, for your patient and tender feedback and support. Thank you, Joseph Gardner, for always making me laugh and always having faith in me. Thank you, Damon Larson, for infusing me with joy and constant motivation to push forward and achieve my goals, and for showing me the type of person I want to be. And thank you, Laura Sierra. You were one of the kindest and most genuine women I've ever known, and you shaped me more than you will ever know. I will always carry your memory in my heart. All of you have impacted my life more than you will ever know, and you did it selflessly, out of nothing but sheer kindness and love for your students. Thank you, thank you, thank you. You are truly the highest class of educators, and I am so grateful for your support of me. I would not be here today without you.

Thank you to all of my friends who read over these passages and offered me feedback, kindness, and support, but especially, thank you, Jack, Val, and Nessa. I was terrified to put this book together and knowing I had people who believed in me gave me a reason to keep going. You mean more to me than you will ever know, and I am immensely grateful for your time and patience. You have given me the strength to put this out into the world.

Thank you to everyone who has read and showed support to me in the past through my Substack publication and through online communities. You have motivated me to keep going, despite everything. You gave me the strength and faith to overcome my fears, and for that, you have my heart forever.

Thank you to my creative inspirations — all the artists, writers, actors, and musicians that have preceded me, which are too many to name. Thank you for making the world more beautiful by the sheer fact of your existence. It takes a lot of bravery and passion to make any kind of art, but you changed my life and inspired me so much. If I'm lucky, I hope to someday do the same with my own creative pursuits.

Most importantly, thank you to all the members of my community, our hallowed species; those who have come before me and will come after, for your strength, vibrance, and bravery to exist. Each and every one of you is important, and you are all so deeply, truly beautiful. Everything I make is (and always will be) devoted to you.

My father told me once that *writing will break your heart, but it will also make you whole.* These days, as the months of work on this book come to a close, I find that it is doing absolutely that. I hope for writing to break my heart for the foreseeable future, because it is the sweetest feeling. I will keep it close to me forever.

Writing and working on this book has consumed me and I have poured out my heart and put years of myself into this work. I realize more and more every day that someday, this book will exist in a place past me — a place in which I can no longer control it. It takes immense bravery to not shelter these works inside my body anymore, but I am happy to let them go. This may be my first book, but I hope it will not be my last, and I hope to one day share my writing with as many as I can. I believe my words are meant to live and breathe beyond me, now. This is the first step to releasing them. They are yours, now.

I know that there are people who will know these words as I do, and I offer every piece in *Ugly Happy* to you. They will only ever be for you, and I hope they speak to you. Please carry them into the world with you as you see fit.

I hope they mean as much to you as they have to me.

This book has now come to close, and I am surrendering it now. It is no longer simply mine, and that is a beautiful, powerful thing. It seems fitting to end this with the passage I cherish most from Tony Kushner's *Angels in America*:

"We won't die secret deaths anymore. The world only spins forward. We will be citizens. The time has come. Bye now. You are fabulous creatures, each and every one.

And I bless you: More Life.

The Great Work Begins."

About the Author

KC Cramm is a 21 year old writer currently studying art history and creative writing. He's not quite sure what he's doing with his life yet, but he hopes to have a good time doing it. He lives in Denver, Colorado. *Ugly Happy* is his first book.